Drawing on real examples from corporate life, as well as anthropological findings, *The Corporate Tribe* shows you:

* How basic tribal principles work in all human groups.
* How your board of directors functions as a council of elders.
* How the power structure of the Akwaaba Tribe is almost identical to the organization chart of a typical corporation.
* How dealing the death blow evolved into closing the sale.
* How the growth of corporations as the major social unit promotes the need for world markets—and decreases the chances of world war.
* How creating corporate totems and ceremonies can strengthen *your* tribe.

"I hope that readers will understand their own corporation better, their role within it, and how to succeed within it. They will also have some new ideas on what's wrong with corporations, why so many people feel frustrated and unfulfilled within them, and what might be done to improve the quality of life within these, our largest and fastest-growing human groups."

—from *The Corporate Tribe*

About the author: A consulting psychologist, Keith D. Wilcock began research into the similarities between corporations and tribes in the early 1970's. He worked as a consultant for ten years with Ernst & Whinney; Booz, Allen & Hamilton; and Peat, Marwick, Mitchell & Co. before establishing his own private practice in 1975. Today he designs and conducts management seminars and provides psychological assessments and career counseling for executives. He also meets with management groups, speaks at conferences on Corporate Tribe concepts, and helps executives define and clarify their archetypal roles.

The Corporate Tribe

Keith D. Wilcock

WARNER BOOKS

A Warner Communications Company

This Warner Books Edition is published by arrangement with
The Wyer-Pearce Press, P.O. Box 219, Excelsior, Minnesota 55331

Cover design by Barbara Buck
Cover photo by Dan Wagner

Warner Books, Inc.
666 Fifth Avenue
New York, N.Y. 10103

Ⓦ A Warner Communications Company

Printed in the United States of America

First Warner Books Printing: December, 1985

10 9 8 7 6 5 4 3 2 1

In memory of Vernile Eyre Wilcock

CONTENTS

ACKNOWLEDGEMENTS 1

FOREWORD 3

1 OUR TRIBAL NATURE 9
Male Bonding — The Pack-Hunting Predator 13
Multiple Tribal Affiliations.. 19
Head Peckers and Pecker Heads 21
Pitfalls in Defining the Pecking Order 30
Bloodless Battles 35
The Ubiquitous Pyramid.. 36
Our Tribal Regalia 42
On a Certain Blindness in Corporate
  Tribesmen.. 44
Some Basic Tribal Principles.. 45

2 TRIBAL TERRITORY..................................... 47
Changes in Food-Getting Knowledge 49
The Happy Hunting Ground 50
An Old Familiar Story.. 53
The Transition to Agriculture...................................... 56
Old Testament Testimony 58
The Emergence of Corporate Tribes............................. 62
The Machine Man.. 64
  The Automobile 65

Television 67
Corporate Nomads 73
Shrinking Family Clusters 75
Territorial Control as a Zero-Sum Game 78
Territory for Corporate Tribes 82
Summary 86

3 ON THE EVOLUTION OF TRIBAL ROLES 87
The Hunter 88
Slavemasters 92
Gatherers 93
The Chief 101
Alpha in Hunting-Gathering Tribes 103
The Chief in Agricultural Tribes 106
The Chief in Corporate Tribes 107
The Passing of the God-Kings 110
Councils of Elders 112
The Headshrinker 114
Evolving Roles 126

4 ON STRENGTHENING CORPORATE TRIBES 129
Commitment 130
Getting the Ax 132
How to Strengthen Your Tribe 134
Fire Fewer Employees 134
Achieve Profit Goals 137
Create More Ceremonies 139
Clarify Tribal Roles 144
Remove Barriers to Corporate Unity 148
Increase Leadership Visibility 150
Encourage Respect for Tribal Elders 152
Create Corporate Totems 153
Give Employees a Piece of the Action 155
A Tribal Builder 156
Wizard Power 160
Current Evolutionary Trends 160

5 ON THE EVOLUTION OF CORPORATE TRIBES 165
Gloom and Doom Prophets 168

What Every Marxist Needs to Know About
    Corporations 173
The New World Tribes 179
Lessons from Allende 181
The Emergence of Third World Corporate
    Tribes 187
Corporate Tribes and War 191
Benevolent Corporations 195
Closing Remarks 198

BIBLIOGRAPHY 203

INDEX 211

THE
CORPORATE
TRIBE

ACKNOWLEDGEMENTS

I wish to express thanks and acknowledge those who helped in the preparation of this book. Judith C. Wilcock, my wife, typed and retyped the manuscript many times. Through several drafts and revisions she patiently did all I asked her to do. Without her efforts and her excellent workmanship the project could not have been completed. Our secretary, Linda Bryant, also provided many hours of typing assistance.

I wish to thank Mr. Gerald J. Barry, of Peat, Marwick, Mitchell & Co. His willingness to publish an early article entitled "The Corporate Tribe" in *World* magazine gave the book-writing project a major push.

Elizabeth White and Neil Raymond were editors who, in the final stages, helped me polish and strengthen the manuscript.

In my search for a publisher, several readers took the time to provide comments and advice. I took all such suggestions seriously.

I also wish to thank my clients and colleagues. Preparing and delivering lectures on *The Corporate Tribe*, speaking at sales conferences and management seminars, responding to questions and listening to discussions have all helped me to better develop the concepts presented in this book.

FOREWORD

ONE day in the late 1960s, I was called into the office of one of Booz, Allen & Hamilton's senior partners. He was the firm's top man in the field of organization studies. As a new Booz Allen consultant, I had been assigned to a project team that would analyze the personnel department of a major bank and recommend to the bank's top management a newly organized personnel function. I was delighted with the assignment. It meant that I would, at last, get the opportunity to learn how one of Booz Allen's top human resources men conducted organization studies.

I studiously reviewed texts and articles on organization theory by Marvin Dunnette, Warren Bennis, Gordon Lippitt, Wendell French, Scott Myers, Chris Argyris, Harry Levinson, Rensis Likert, and Frederick Hertzberg. I wanted to be prepared.

The meeting with the Booz Allen partner lasted about fifteen minutes. No organization theory was discussed. We went away with a small pencil sketch on a piece of scratch paper. Three months later the sketch would appear again, beautifully rendered by Booz Allen's graphics department. A report, complete with chapters and well-organized dot-point headings, accompanied the chart.

The bank was delighted with the organization study. Its officers paid our bill promptly and followed most of our recommendations.

But a nagging feeling of frustration stayed with me. I had expected to learn some amazing secrets, some arcane and wonderful clues to understanding how corporations should be organized. I had expected to be able to apply my training as an industrial psychologist. Instead, it seemed that Booz Allen's seasoned approach to organization studies was based, almost completely, on common sense.

I suppose most executives tend to romanticize about the mysteries of fields they know little about. Data processing, finance and corporate taxation seem mysterious from a distance. But when one finally gets exposed, as I did in the Booz Allen organization study, the mist evaporates leaving one wondering why it seemed so intriguing in the first place.

It has been over twenty years since I began to work as a consulting psychologist in industry. During that time, I have worked with about 100 corporations. These clients have included large organizations with over a billion dollars in sales, and small ones. They include manufacturing companies, food companies, a railroad, three airlines, several banks and savings and loan associations, a number of not-for-profit service and professional organizations, partnerships, universities, and a variety of government organizations.

My early experience with Booz Allen has been replayed dozens of times. One corporation after another seems to run on a kind of common sense automatic pilot. They solve problems, formulate policies and resolve employee controversies without paying much attention to organization theorists. They do what seems right. Throughout the past 20 years I have felt there was a great deal going on within corporations that was not fully understood.

As a consultant, I was in the position of being exposed to corporations that differed dramatically in the products and services they supplied. Yet there was an amazing amount of internal similarity from one organization to another. All had dominance hierarchies. All had a top leader. These persons went by a variety of titles. They were called CEO, executive director, chairman of the board, managing partner, governor, general manager and warden, as well as president. But all were acknowledged as performing the top leadership role. All but one were men. Most had similar departments such as sales, production, accounting and personnel. These groups varied in size, but their functions, from one company to another, were very similar. All of the large corporations I observed had separate pay programs for hourly, salaried, and executive employees. All had similar operating practices and personnel policies. These similarities impressed me as being more than a coincidence.

Some of my consulting engagements with these clients lasted only a week or two. Others involved the use of my services on and off for many years. Almost all of them have provided exposure to top management executives and decision making at the policy level.

Like other psychologists in industry, I have spent thousands of hours thinking about organizations, how they work, how to stimulate motivation and productivity within the work force, how to improve work environments, how to strengthen employment, recruiting and the process of management succession, how to identify and develop leadership and mangement talent and how to strengthen team effort. Most of all I have wondered, "What are corporations? How do they fit into our rapidly growing knowledge of man's evolution?"

Psychologists are just about the only behavioral scientists who find careers in big business, and they do not always enjoy a sparkling reputation. Many are regarded as "far out." Others are seen as too academic, ivory tower or impractical. There is an undercurrent of mistrust among managers, particularly about sensitivity training and psychological testing.

Where psychologists are often mistrusted, other major fields of the behavioral sciences have little or no impact on corporations. Thus far in my field work among corporations, I have met no sociologists and no anthropologists who were actively pursuing professional careers within business.

The result is that few businessmen know much about how the recent findings of cultural anthropologists, ethologists or archeologists might apply to them. And conversely, not many researchers in these fields of the behavioral sciences know much about big business.

Anthropologists seem to have avoided careers in modern business corporations. They work for universities and research foundations. "Send me to the frontier," they cry. The more primitive, the better. They feel sad about there being no more new tribes to discover. "Give me dirty trousers and whiskers!" they bellow.

A business suit? A tie? Shave every morning? 8:00 AM to work every day, cities, pollution, commuting, the Wall Street Journal, suburbia — blech! And because anthropologists have stayed away from corporations, few bridges have been built.

In fact, some anthropologists seemed to have defined corporations as the bad guys. Many espouse ominous Marxists and socialist notions.

Anthropologists are correct to insist on extensive field work before presuming to write about primitive tribes. But very few anthropologists have done enough in-depth field work within corporate organizations to write authoritatively about them. They prefer primitive tribes, and the few who have attempted to generalize from their field work in the bush sound academic. Corporate managers are quick to recognize and dismiss academic treatises. They have endured a substantial quantity of dung-throwing from the ivory towers. To be convincing, one must speak in the language of the corporate manager.

In a sense, anthropologists have painted themselves into a corner. Having vehemently insisted on field work, they are now facing increasing resistance from governments of so-called primitive tribes. Opportunities for field work are increasingly difficult to find. Perhaps *The Corporate Tribe* will help open some doors so that anthropologists will have a few more opportunities to consult with major corporations. I would be delighted to see Corporate Anthropology included in the class offerings of a few major universities.

Part of the role of the applied scientist is to attempt to translate new research results into practical, understandable and useable programs. I attempt to do this for the corporations who use my services. This book is another attempt.

I believe that references to specific individuals and corporations in the book are sufficiently disguised to avoid embarrassing any of the organizations which were kind enough to retain me.

Readers should not assume that any of my clients would agree with opinions and arguments in *The Corporate Tribe*. For better or worse, they are my own.

Where did corporations come from anyway? Did they emerge brand new, or are they an outgrowth of prior organization forms?

How and why do certain individuals become president? How much do we know about the adult roles of males and females in mammal herds, in the primate clusters closely related to man, among pack-hunting predators, in tribes throughout the world and back into pre-history? Do elements of hunting and gathering still exist in corporate activities?

Will corporations survive? What can we learn from the survival struggles of primitive tribes that might make modern corporations better and stronger?

These are elementary questions. They are vital to all executives.

I apologize in advance for the occasional leaps into speculation on the basis of the first early scraps of evidence about evolving human organizations. Some of the views expressed in the book are probably wrong. Someone will come along and disprove them. But I think many of the views are right. Future research will confirm them.

My reason for writing this book is not complicated. I feel that a better understanding of corporate tribology will help all corporate employees to strengthen their companies, and by so doing, help them to survive and grow.

I feel that my research into the tribal nature of corporations has given me a valuable perspective. It has helped me to more clearly understand important issues regarding corporate objectives, organization and management succession. It has proven valuable in individual career counseling as well as in the analysis and formulation of corporate policy. It has also helped me to clarify and more effectively contribute to the essential objectives of my client corporations. I feel that I know and understand corporations far better now than when my research began. My counsel and advice is more clear, more useful, and more likely to contribute to the survival and growth of my client tribes.

And there are broader benefits, beyond those of strengthening the survival capabilities and growth of a few client corporations. By clarifying the evolutionary process, we may be able to better understand the direction of corporate evolution.

I am hopeful that the corporate employees and executives who read *The Corporate Tribe* will start to see their companies in a new, more healthy, more optimistic way. I feel my own opinions about corporations have become more optimistic as my research progressed.

I hope that readers will understand their own corporation better, their role within it, and how to succeed within it. They will also have some new ideas on what's wrong with corporations, why so many people feel frustrated and unfulfilled within them, and what might be done to improve the quality of life within these, our largest and fastest-growing human groups.

Chapter One

❖

OUR TRIBAL NATURE

IN the 1960s and 70s, careful observations of animals in the wild began to reveal new information regarding herd behavior. To the casual observer, all the animals of a given herd may look alike. As scientists began to identify individual animals and record daily interactions within the herds, it became apparent that the clustered animals were not simply a random mass of milling beasts. Their movements seemed to follow basic patterns and principles. When the existence of pecking orders and dominance hierarchies within animal clusters was discovered, interactions within herds or flocks could no longer be regarded as random.

It became clear that principles or laws were working which tended to result in predictable and intricate patterns of interaction. The behavior of clustered animals was organized. The exact way the clusters were organized, for example, the number of individuals in a cluster, differed from one species to another. But within a given species, the interactions and organization structures were alike. Further observation suggests that the manner in which various individuals react and relate to one another within a given group or cluster contributes to the survival of the herd. Not only do birds of a feather flock together, flocks of a feather survive together.

How long have various species been forming their characteristic clusters? How long have lions formed prides with one adult male and several adult females? How long have stallions and walruses formed harems? How long have baboons been forming troops with a dominant male and several powerful "lieutenants" who help keep the pecking order in place? If these species-specific clusters are essential to survival, they have probably existed for thousands, perhaps millions of years.

Alas, man is no exception. Like other animals, we survive in clusters. We form herds. Each day we swarm. Each night the swarms disperse. We are gregarious animals. We work, worship, play and make war in clusters.

The human clusters we see around us today, like other animal clusters, have existed with similar internal organization for tens of thousands, perhaps millions of years. Further, the roles of individuals within these structures, the ways that individuals operate, organize and divide work, probably contribute to the group's survival and growth. These fundamental roles may be far older than we have previously imagined. They may be essential to our survival as animals.

All over the world, one generation after another, one observes a great many similarities and consistencies in these human clusters. I have come to believe, like others, that all human groups abide by ancient laws of nature and that what we call corporations are, in fact, modern-day tribes.

To apply Darwin's wonderful tree metaphor to human groups, corporations might be the leaves. The armies, churches and village governments of the 10,000-year agricultural era, from which corporations so recently evolved, are the twigs and branches. The trunk from which all else has grown is the hunting-gathering tribe. As so many have pointed out, we humans were hunters and gatherers for over 90% of our anthropological history.

Homo sapiens, like other animals, live in clusters—in groups. We are a kind of herd or pack animal, and we do not organize randomly. Like ants, bees, termites, birds and other mammals, Homo sapiens organize in predictable clusters.

It is not a coincidence that all corporations are organized in pyramid-shaped dominance hierarchies. These organized clusters have probably existed for millions of years. They are tribes.

The central thesis of this book is that modern corporations are evolved tribes. They are mutations. In many ways they are still firmly locked in a multi-million-year-old groove of tribal evolution. In other ways they are new—different from anything that has gone before.

Jung believed that all of us carry certain subconscious memories with us as dispositions to act. They may be elements of the "collective unconscious," part of our anthropological history. He referred to them as "archetypes." These archetypes sort of glow in deeper centers of our brains, until experiences, serving as releasing mechanisms, bring them forth. He felt they also come forth spontaneously in dream images. He identified several such archetypes, including Anima, the female archetype, and Animus, the male archetype.

The newly emerging realization that we are tribal beasts, dramatically expands the list of archetypes. It is becoming clear that the tribal roles of chief, hunter, elder, gatherer and shaman are also archetypal. They have existed, generation after generation, for millions of years.

Although my business card reads Licensed Consulting Psychologist, my clients call me a "headshrinker." The term is more accurate than they realize. The role I play with the companies I serve is essentially the same as that of a shaman in primitive tribes. The role is archetypal. It appears in primitive and modern tribes in Africa, Asia, North and South America, Europe, the Pacific Islands—in short, wherever men are found. The title changes from tribe to tribe. We are called brujos, fetishers, medicine men, witch doctors, high priests, wizards and magicians.

We have special knowledge which can help the tribe survive and prosper.

In 1970, when I began to seriously study the relationships between modern corporations and primitive tribes, I had no idea that my role was both ancient and common to all tribes. I believed that consulting psychologists were a rather new and modern phenomenon. But as my research progressed, it became clear to me that all corporate employees are fulfilling archetypal roles. The salesman is the evolved hunter. The factory worker is the evolved slave. The president is alpha—the dominant male—the chief. The Board of Directors is the evolved Council of Elders. Secretaries, receptionists and file clerks are evolved gatherers.

We are all tribesmen and tribeswomen. All of our jobs can be traced to the earlier tribal roles.

The news that corporations are evolved tribes is not likely to surprise many anthropologists. A rather large number of scientists, as early as Freud[1] and Jung[2] have already described man's tribal nature. Marx[3] described elements of it. Herbert Spenser[4] compiled extensive comparisons of primitive tribes. Several early corporate barons described themselves as "Social Darwinists." Lionel Tiger's *Men in Groups*[5] greatly clarified it. Journalists such as Anthony Jay[6] *(Corporation Man)* have made valuable observations. The recent book entitled *Corporate Cultures*, by Deal and Kennedy,[7] pried open the doors of understanding a little wider. But most of the business executives I work with on a daily basis are both surprised and fascinated by the information.

There are many obvious differences between primitive tribes and corporations. Such things as clothing, hair styles, building designs and materials, religious beliefs and art forms vary from tribe to tribe. But there are also many similarities, not always so obvious. They suggest that modern corporate organizations are evolving tribes.

Male Bonding - The Pack-Hunting Predator

Male bonding, simply stated, is a tendency of males to bunch together. According to Lionel Tiger, who has written the authoritative text on the subject, male bonding occurs in all human societies[8]. Corporate management groups, without doubt, provide clear examples of male bonding. Tiger suggests that male bonding is instinctual in Homo sapiens, a species-specific behavior. Almost all adult men everywhere, including all of our ancestors, were associated with these all-male clusters, and as such, they shared many of the same experiences of modern men in corporations. All men, alive and dead, have dealt with and been influenced by these male clusters.

When did male bonding first emerge? John Hurrel Crook's studies of "Cooperation in Primates" suggests:

> *"The development of two types of society in ground dwelling monkeys is linked with the increasing aridity of Africa in post pleistocene times and the spread of savannah and semi-desert conditions. In both these societies there is evidence of some carnivorous propensity ... In the open savannah of Africa in the pleistocene, the biomass of grass eating mammals (ungulates, etc.) was such to encourage exploitation by capable predators. Tool-using protohominids at a chimpanzee grade of social organization, forced to live in environments harsher than fruit-bearing forests of open woodland, would rapidly have acquired the taste for meat and the weapons for obtaining it. The change may well have been associated with the development of 'all-male groups' (known in chimpanzees and gelada baboons, for example) into hunting parties and the institution of settlements in protective sleeping places formerly abandoned during the day-ranging of the groups."[9]*

So the relationship between bonding and hunting-defense activities may have emerged as apelike prehistoric men adjusted gradually to the grasslands that replaced receding forests and jungles. The gradual change in climate resulted in corresponding changes in food supply. This favored certain life forms and was fatal to others.

Changes in climate favored the emergence of grasslands. The grass-eating animals flourished and, in turn, became food for predators, including early man. Evidence from hundreds of digs strongly suggests that prehistoric males were pack-hunting predators. Females were gatherers, and they too worked in bonded groups. All able-bodied adults searched for food, but the female groups often accounted for a larger percentage, by weight, of the total food consumed.

For at least six million years, males hunted in adult groups. Seen as a simple conditioning process, the act of killing immediately preceding the act of eating, might come to function like Pavlov's bell. To eat, to survive, meant to kill.

Those who track the prehistoric development of Homo sapiens suggest that male bonding had clear survival value. Men were smaller, slower and weaker than many of the animals they hunted in prehistoric times, therefore, hunting teams were more successful than individual hunters. And early tribes which could successfully obtain food survived better, lived longer, fathered more offspring and were better equipped to keep their offspring alive. So the genetic traits of men who bonded were probably transmitted with greater reliability than the traits of those who broke away from the pack and tried to make it on their own. Individual hunters and gatherers may be less successful feeding themselves or their offspring. It is clear that they would be less able to defend themselves or their offspring from predators. If either the individual or his offspring died because of starvation or predators, genetic transmission of his traits would cease.

The addition of another key factor dramatically strengthens the impact of male and female bonding on genetic transmission. Man's most dangerous predator has always been other men, and in most cases the smaller or weaker group loses. When a predatory raiding party sets forth, its victims are often smaller groups, or individuals. It is easy to see how killing the males of smaller and weaker tribes by larger, smarter, or stronger groups of cooperative predators may have had the effect of gradually upgrading the quality of each succeeding human generation.

Paleontologists point to evidence which shows a significant expansion of early man's cranial capacity during the period when males adapted to pack-hunting and began to refine their predatory skills.

But there were other reasons why early men and women may have bonded. In addition to their gathering activities, the women kept having babies, producing new tribespeople, as if by magic. The female produced children for her clan, her totem. Gods worked within her. The men were merely observers.

Malinowski discovered that the Trobriand Islanders knew nothing about the male role in creating babies. To them, sex and childbirth were unrelated. New people came from gods through women of the tribe. All tribes people traced their lineage through women.[10]

Jane Goodall indicates that chimpanzee families are composed only of a mother and children. There are no real "father" roles as we know them. "In fact," says Goodall, "neither we nor the chimpanzees normally have any idea as to which male was responsible for siring which child." Female chimpanzees in heat mate with many males.[11]

Adult male chimpanzees form all male clusters. They develop pyramid-shaped dominance hierarchies. There is a dominant male, several sub-dominants, then a layer of younger adults and older males past their prime. They spend major portions of their day separated from the company of females and children, who form a separate group.

In his chapter on Comparative Family Patterns, Robin Fox states,

> *"In some primitive hunting groups, the total pattern is still very like that of primates: the females and young stay pretty much together as a group; the adult (initiated) males follow their own pursuits, the adolescent (uninitiated) males form a peripheral set."*[12]

Over the last six million years, when did people in tribes here and there around the world begin to discover that men

help to create babies? There is reason to believe it may have
happened sometime during the conversion from hunting and
gathering to agriculture.

Just as with other higher primates, early hunting-gathering
tribes which were matrilineal left the males detached from fam-
ilial responsibilities. They formed all-male clusters. Males of
some Amazon basin tribes still sleep in a common men's hut.
In some tribes these male clusters lived significant portions of
their lives apart from the company of women and children.
There were no families as we know them, no father roles, and
in some tribes, no knowledge of the male role in creating
babies—no realization for any of the men that "that child, the
one with the dimples, is mine."

Marriage and the concept of family undoubtedly changed
when a man and woman could finally say, "These are our
children", when the father role emerged, when males at last
realized that they too had children. Prior to the emergence of
families, the totem group captured the primary loyalty of both
men and women.

The patrilineal tribes, along with the concepts of father and
a male creator, may have emerged with agriculture and with
new knowledge of conception necessary for the breeding and
domestication of animals.

The change from hunting and gathering to agriculture resulted in a change in family structure. The family, as we know
it, may be a relatively recent development, perhaps less than
20,000 years old.

All male clusters, like those observed in corporate management, may be older than families as we know them. All male
clusters were and are common in matrilineal tribes. They continued to be found in the armies, governments, churches, and
work groups of agricultural tribes, and they surfaced intact
during the recent emergence of corporations.

The significance of male bonding is just beginning to come
into focus. Now that Tiger has pointed it out, it seems obvious.

But we have somehow been blind to the obvious.

Until the 1960s, most animal studies were drawn from observations made in zoos. The cages created artificial, highly restricted territories. To avoid clashes or conflicts, male animals were separated. Thus, male interaction and relationships were artificially eliminated. Animals in zoos had no natural predators and their diets were atypical. Under these conditions, normal social processes were disrupted. The understanding of such phenomenon as male bonding, territorial behavior and pecking orders, began to take form only recently when scientists recognized the importance of studying animals in their natural environments.

The significance of male bonding also failed to be recognized because during the 1940s and 50s, maternal behavior monopolized the attention of so many behavioral scientists. Freud focused attention on mother-child relationships in early development, and when the efforts of modern science were focused on maternal behavior, a rich body of fascinating new information emerged that dominated the attention of behavioral scientists. Like treasure seekers, we have been so mesmerized by the beauty of the first jewels to be unearthed, we failed to notice other nearby treasures. Male and female bonding may be other jewels, ones that offer rich rewards for those researchers skilled enough to unearth the full impact of their meaning.

Male and female bonding are greatly encouraged among the children and adolescents of both modern and primitive man. During kindergarten, at age five, the pattern of boys playing with boys, and girls with girls, is already well established. Adolescent boys' and girls' groups, such as sports teams, Boy Scouts, Girl Scouts, fraternities, sororities, and all male street gangs, can be found in cultures which are widely separated in geography, religion and customs. Young boys and girls of approximately the same age form sexually segregated clusters.

Observations suggest that such bonding continues, unabated, from early childhood to old age. The average executive has actively participated in bonded clusters throughout his or her life.

*   *   *

Freddie Jones played with the boys in kindergarten. He joined Cub Scouts at age 8. He also played on a Little League baseball team. At age 12 he graduated to Boy Scouts and played both baseball and hockey. At age 14 he began to spend an increasing number of hours per day with his boy-friends, in addition to the organized sports and church ac-tivities. In high school Fred continued to be active in sports. Three of his school classes were all boys—industrial arts, physical education and ROTC. He walked to school with male friends and ate lunch with them.

As he grew older, depending on his socio-economic level, he joined a street gang, the army or a fraternity. If he went to college, many of his classes—in law school, business administration, athletics, ROTC, engineering, pre-med—were nearly 100% male. For two years in the Army he was immersed again in all-male group activities.

The girls in Freddie's life formed a counterpoint of female-bonded groups, such as Brownies, Girls Scouts, cheerleaders and sororities. So modern children are well conditioned for their adult experiences in sex-segregated groups.

When Freddie begins his career in the corporate tribe, a similar pattern continues. He works with men, eats lunch with men, has meetings with men, works on boards and committees with men. The male-operating clusters at upper levels of corporate management associate with females, but women are most frequently given roles as secretaries and clerical office employees.

*   *   *

Clusters of females in typing pools, processing checks in banks, working as reservation agents in airlines, or in sewing operations in textile mills, are modern examples of bonded-female working groups. Women are seldom included in the top-level councils and have limited direct impact on corporate decision making. In this respect, their role may parallel that of gatherers in earlier tribes.

Multiple Tribal Affiliations

Our appetite for tribal activity is so great that even weekend and evening activity is often devoted to it. Most modern men and women have several tribal affiliations. The corporation provides our daytime, food-getting occupation. On Sunday we go to churches. These too are tribes, governed by all-male, pyramid-shaped dominance hierarchies. In all our modern enlightenment we still observe and participate in most of the same ceremonies that occupied the tribal life of earlier men and women. Most marriages, funerals and infant-naming ceremonies still take place in a tribal situation. These religious tribes struggle for territory, for growth in membership and financial resources, as actively and urgently as other tribes.

Political organizations also form tribes. City, county, state and national governments, including the organizations for the services they offer — such as police and fire protection, road maintenance and national defense — all are organized into the same basic pyramid-shaped units. Citizens of the political territories who provide taxes to pay for those services are essentially contributing to a political tribe. A vote is a form of tribal membership. It represents a voice in some politically-defined territory.

With this perspective, our multiple tribal affiliations are more clearly seen. Our largest and most powerful tribes are usually our nation states. Men are still called upon to kill or be killed to defend these patches of territory, as the Falkland Islands, Grenada and the conflict in Lebanon recently demonstrated. Nation-state armies provide a protective umbrella, under which thousands of churches, schools, hospitals and corporations attempt to flourish.

TV provides a powerful new window which tends to tune us into various tribal arenas and activities. Marshall McLuhan referred to it as "the global village."[13] National and international news as well as local stories provide a fascinating opportunity to participate in truly gigantic tribal events. TV has provided an electronic substitute for many of the tribal meetings, ceremonies and entertainments that used to occupy the evening and special holiday activities of hunter-gatherers.

Singing and dancing long into the night, was one of the great joys of earlier tribes. The evenings of modern men are similarly occupied. But as members of the TV tribe we participate only as an audience. Still, the quality, variety and educational impact of movies and television programs makes them powerful transmitters and interpreters of our modern tribal values, perhaps even more effective than the story tellers or the costumed and masked singers and dancers of earlier tribes.

Our modern tribal heros and heroines are played by Hollywood stars. Our tribal warriors are now athletes who perform a fascinating variety of symbolic territorial struggles for our entertainment.

Much of the analysis presented in this book will apply to all kinds of tribes. But the focus is "corporate tribes", a type of tribe that absorbs eight or more prime hours a day, five or six days a week, for millions of adult Homo sapiens.

In earlier tribes the hunting, religious ceremonies and political events all took place with the same cast of friends and relatives. For modern man, our various tribal affiliations have become scattered and compartmentalized, but we still conduct the events of our daily lives and our various tribal activities and ceremonies much like earlier men and women.

There are no children in corporate tribes. Corporations are composed exclusively of adults. Before a child is eligible to become an employee, he or she must go through a rites-of-passage ceremony. For modern business men and women, this is known as commencement. High school and trade school graduation allow entry into blue-collar jobs. Most of those who aspire to management must also graduate from college. College commencement is a tribal rites-of-passage into corporate management. The strange robes, tassled hats and colored sashes are traditional tribal costumes of our modern rites-of-passage. Now, as in earlier tribes, they grant permission to join the hunt.

For most adult males, corporate activities have essentially taken the place of hunting and war. The hunt was the normal daytime food-getting activity of adult males for millions of years. At periodic intervals the quarry changed from animals to other men, the activity from hunting to war.

Child rearing and gathering were the normal daytime activities of women. Much of their time was spent in clusters made up of females and children. Recognizing that much corporation activity is the evolved hunt helps to explain why it is a serious, high-pressure, survival-oriented activity. To hunt, one must be fit. To wage war, one must be fit. Perhaps it also explains why military analogies are so compelling, and so often used in describing corporate activity.

Recognizing that corporations represent evolved hunting-and-gathering clusters also helps clarify why the profit motive has withstood so much abuse from critics of modern corporations. To the corporate tribe, profit is food. It is meat. It is the spoils of war. It represents the capacity to grow—to increase wealth, expand territory and increase the number of employees. It represents tribal survival.

Head Peckers and Pecker Heads

During the Spring of 1971, I accompanied a group of old-bird executives on a fishing trip to Canada. The trip was an annual event, and I felt its success was due largely to the informal traditions that had arisen. The group usually consisted of eight to ten men, two to a boat during the day.

The shore lunches were an intriguing display of pecking order in action. New members of the party, myself included, performed the menial tasks—gathering wood, peeling potatoes, etc. More experienced men would select the campsite and build the fire. The veterans turned the morning's catch into fillets, and prepared the coffee.

The most responsible job was preparing the fried potatoes. The job fell to a seasoned old Dutchman, a veteran of many campaigns. No one was able to match his recipe. The potatoes, with bacon and onions, all burnt almost to charcoal and dripping with grease, were delicious.

We traded fishing buddies each day, and one day I ended up with a man who had recently decided to take early retirement. During the long afternoon, when the fish were not biting, he told me an amazing story.

I will call him Jim. He was an aggressive, powerful man. His influence in the group was immense, because of his intelligence, his booming voice (he loved to sing Ivan Skavinski Skavar with gusto), and his natural leadership capabilities.

Jim had risen to power in a big eight public accounting partnership. He had responsibility for management services, the newest and fastest-growing segment of the business. Revenues and staff had grown dramatically under his leadership. His power and influence had also grown to the point where he had become a major contender for the top position—alpha—the chief.

Large partnerships are unique. In many ways they parallel the organization forms of the Plains Indians of North America. A new chief is selected by a vote. Each sub-chief accumulates voting shares on the basis of his position in the pecking order.

Jim lost his bid for chief. Another man had accumulated more votes among powerful sub-chiefs.

The events that followed show one way the pecking order operates at top levels of modern organizations. Five years had elapsed since Jim had lost his bid for top dog.

As we sat, listening to the trolling motor throb quietly and the water lap gently against the sides of the boat, he confided to me that in five years he had never had a single business conversation with the man who had defeated him. He had simply been cut off from communication. One by one, his loyal lieutenants were transferred away from him. The men he recommended for promotions were passed over.

For five years his life had been miserable, even though I would estimate his income to have been well over $300,000 per year.

Occasionally he presented his ideas and plans before groups of colleagues in meetings. But his advice or opinions were never solicited, and his written requests and recommendations were never returned to him.

Finally Jim could take no more. He was miserable. One by one the strings of his power had been snipped. He started thinking seriously about retirement.

After our shore lunches were over and we had shoved our boats off from shore, the seagulls would arrive. The competition for scraps of food was intense, but always, when the dominant bird arrived, the others would scatter.

Jim saw the parallels. "See that one? That's the head pecker," he would say, identifying the obviously dominant bird. "The rest are pecker heads."

The competitive struggle for food scraps among the seagulls was a clear example of the pecking order in action. So was the breakdown of responsibilities during the shore lunch. No one really assigned duties, but all of the men were keenly aware of the subtle pressures and traditions that were operating. I would never have been so insane as to start cooking the potatoes.

On one occasion a new man on the trip set up a small frying pan on the edge of the grill to prepare a grilled cheese sandwich. Because he had stepped out of line he had a rough time. His pan got moved a couple of times to make room for higher priority items, such as water for the coffee. Someone accidentally kicked some ashes into his pan.

To be generous he prepared an extra sandwich and invited others to share. The extra sandwich lay there in the frying pan, getting cold and soggy. In the end it was tossed in the campfire with the potato peelings and coffee grounds. When the men moved out, the head pecker among the seagulls took charge and claimed the morsel for himself.

Of course, Jim was a pecker head too. At least he had not achieved the head pecker status in his firm. He was like one of the large, powerful birds who sits on the outskirts of the action until the head pecker has had his fill and leaves the field. He was still pecking off his $300,000 per year, and few of the lesser birds would dare to challenge him, but he knew he would lose a direct confrontation with the head pecker, and so did everyone else.

Like male bonding, the significance of "pecking order" in groups of animals and men is a relatively recent discovery. Observation of chickens reveals that the dominant chicken in a flock pecks whomever she chooses—a hard, sharp whack on the top of the head. The second most dominant pecks anyone but the top chicken. The third most dominant pecks all but the top two, and so forth. Through an ongoing process of challenges and conflict resolutions, a pecking order is defined.

Since the principle was first discovered, pecking orders have been observed in a wide variety of birds and mammals.

For certain primates, including chimpanzees and baboons, the dominant male rules with active assistance from one or two vice-presidents. In this way, he extends his reign far past his prime of physical strength.

Tinbergen[14] demonstrated that young geese learn about position in the pecking order from their mothers. Goslings of a dominant goose will win confrontations with goslings of subordinate geese. However, a reshuffling takes place when the goslings mature, become independent, and mark off their own territories.

The relationship between the pecking order and genetic transmission was eloquently portrayed by Robert Ardrey in *The Territorial Imperative*.[15] He described studies by Helmut K. Buechnes about the Uganda Kob, a type of antelope. Careful observations of the Kob reveal that only the strongest males, perhaps twelve to fifteen from a herd of eight hundred or a thousand, perform the breeding function for the entire herd. They do it on a strange bit of territory referred to as a stamping ground. According to Ardrey, the stamping ground is a collection of putting greens, each about fifty feet diameter, and each defended by a single male.

"Here the champion males ... a kind of sexual olympic team—fight, display and jockey for position. Here needy females come seeking consolation".[16]

Ardrey goes on to say that within the arena of putting greens, a territorial pyramid emerges.

"Young ambitious males fight for a foothold on the periphery ... They wait for an opening, challenge, and fight to gain better, more central locations. And on a few central territories—perhaps only three or four—stand the champions of the moment, challenged by all, desired by every female heart."[17]

Males who do not gain a breeding ground appear to be sexually unmotivated, and females are correspondingly unresponsive to them.

The strongest males have an amazingly active sex life. Females are drawn to the central breeding grounds of the dominant males, and usually pass through the peripheral territories to munch the close-cropped grass of the champions——an act which triggers the breeding ritual. Ardrey observed one champion who "resisted five challenges in an hour and a half, and a twenty-minute horn-locked pushing contest that left him scarcely able to stand. Yet, the doe, despite her apparent fragility, may, in full sweep of estrus, demand copulation ten times in a day."

The result of this rigorous process is that a small number of the strongest, most dominant males, the most impressive heroes, are selected to contribute their genetic characteristics to the herd's offspring. The majority of males have no offspring. They contribute nothing to the next generation of Kobs.

Jane Goodall's field observations of baboons show that dominance is seldom achieved in the same troop in which a young male was reared. There comes a time when mature young males strike out on their own. When they achieve their full adult growth they find a new troop and literally fight their way into the pecking order.

Goodall captured one such episode on film.

*   *   *

One day a large male was observed strolling alone down the beach toward an established troop of baboons. Although he violated the troop's territory he did not attempt to enter the troop for several days.

His presence caused tension among the males, but when he stopped a safe distance from the troop it subsided.

The newcomer bided his time, watched the activities of the troop carefully. He appeared to be studying the troop to determine how far up into the pecking order he could move.

When he made his move he strode boldly into the heart of the troop. First he intimidated a couple of young maturing males. They refused to fight and soon assumed subordinate postures, indicating they would yield to him. He then picked out a stronger but aging male, one that had recently lost a couple of notches on the pecking order. The newcomer threatened and crowded the older male until he ran from the confrontation.

Having demonstrated his ability to frighten the young and older males he strode directly into the top ranks of the pecking order.

Two high-ranking males joined forces to engage him. Biting and tearing with their claws, they battled for several minutes. Finally, the newcomer was able to divide his attackers and, one at a time, defeat them.

The newcomer took over the number two position in the troop. After displacing his opponents he approached the dominant male, turned his hindquarters in a deference gesture, and received the ritual grooming. The dominant male was in effect saying, "Good fight. Nice to have you aboard."

Often such fights result in a chain reaction of violent clashes, a clear domino effect which subsides only when the new pecking order is set in place. Each male reasserts his dominance over those below him. Many times the young and females take substantial abuse from frustrated adult males who lose a notch in status.

The newcomer, in this instance, had left a troop, found a new one and forced his way into a position of power.

★   ★   ★

In *The Territorial Imperative* Ardrey makes the point that challengers rarely win direct confrontations with individuals who hold superior positions in the pecking order.[18] Position in the pecking order is related to territory within the tribe, and once an individual gains control of a given territory, he holds a powerful psychological advantage. This principle clearly operates in the corporate tribe.

The naive young executive who threatens to quit if he does not get his way very frequently receives a sharp peck on the head. He gets fired. The perceptive young manager understands that advancement in the pecking order rarely occurs without support from above.

★   ★   ★

Steve Anderson was a young, confident, aggressive executive. His attire revealed an impeccable attention to style. He made most decisions with ease. He was intelligent, independent and quick to assume the initiative. He was vice president of a corporate division that was struggling. He had helped with an active cost-cutting program that had moved the division from a $300,000 loss position into the black. During the second year his division missed its $250,000 profit target substantially. It managed to stay in the black, but only after a full year of hectic fire-fighting. When corporate leaders decided to replace Steve's boss, Steve was one of two plausible candidates.

In spite of his record, Steve was not chosen, and the reason sheds light on a common but unwritten custom of the corporate tribe.

Many young warriors blow themselves out. Rather than display deference (the young male baboon shivers and shows his ass when approaching the dominant male), some aggressive young executives naively challenge the existing authority. If and when he does this, his chances for success are slim.

Steve's mistake was refusing to attend an assessment center. He believed he should be evaluated on the basis of measured results. He had been through psychological testing with a previous corporation and the process infuriated him. He was asked to participate in the assessment center by the vice-president of personnel. He hesitated. Then his immediate superior urged him to attend. He explained his position and asked to be considered for the promotion on the basis of his track record. The decision sealed his doom. He did not know it for several months but the attitudes of the corporate leaders froze him out. One day he was called in and given two months to find another job.

★   ★   ★

The rules which govern this type of activity operate as unwritten policies. The head chiefs could no more articulate the principles behind their actions than the head baboon who explodes in rage and bites the ear off some brash youngster who challenges him. And the process is replayed wherever male beasts live together.

I remember my first day in a corporate tribe. I had been hired by a prestigious national public accounting firm—one of the big eight.

Early on the first day I was given a tour of my new tribal village. At the end of the hall we passed a sort of shrine, a carved wooden table with a pair of candelabra under a large darkly painted oil portrait.

"This is J. William Crossman," the tour guide said reverently, "one of the founders. He's dead now."

He was there in full tribal regalia: dark double-breasted suit, vest, gold watch chain, diamond ring and the same authoritative expression one sees on the photographed faces of American Indian chiefs. The personnel man began to speak in hushed tones as we approached "partners row." The offices were impressive. They were large. The floor-to-ceiling wood paneling was rich, Elizabethan looking. The executive men's room had cloth towels and a shoeshine machine. We also took a quick, obsequious peek at the managing partner's office. Situated in a corner of the building, it had a panoramic view of the city. It was larger and better furnished than any of the other offices. I didn't fully realize the importance of the windows, carpet, drapes, desk size, furniture and potted plants at the time, but soon after I started, the consulting division where I was employed was moved. Only then did I discover the significance of office space and furnishings.

Partners were given a decorating budget and allowed to select drapes and carpeting. They had potted plants, large desks, credenzas and a long list of other items. Managers received a shorter, but well-defined list of furnishings. Then came supervisors, and finally the troops.

One day I brought a small ivy plant to sit on my corner of a shared bookcase. A more senior tribesman cornered me and with a grave expression suggested that my ivy plant may seem a bit ostentatious, since only partners were allowed plants. As the plant grew so did the annoyance and discomfort of those who had been so meticulous in attempting to structure the pecking order.

After nineteen years of consulting assignments in corporate organizations I discovered that my firm was much like other corporate tribes. On various client visits I observed dozens of shrines for dead chiefs, spacious corner huts for headmen, nearby huts for sub-chiefs and carefully worked-out symbols which identify a given tribesman's position in the organization.

Pitfalls in Defining the Pecking Order

Sometimes it is difficult to accurately define the pecking order in a corporate tribe. This is especially true for outsiders and new members of the tribe. But if the new man accidentally violates another executive's territory, the pecking order machinery grinds into motion. It clanks and clatters and runs its course, and when it finishes the pecking order is once again in place. Usually the new man is humbled. Sometimes he is fired. He usually has a clearer picture of the pecking order and where he stands in it.

★   ★   ★

A major university had actively sought out a new dean for its law school. The board had insisted on finding a young, innovative, forward-thinking man, one the students would like. The best candidate was interviewed and found to be acceptable, but he was skeptical of the offer. He had been dreaming of a different career path with a more prestigious university, but the people he talked with were persuasive. He would have a free hand, could build his own kind of school, select his own staff. With that incentive, he accepted.

The law school, like so many others around the country, had doubled its enrollment in recent years and had outgrown its present facility. Students were crammed into every closet.

The young dean, without realizing that he was treading on the semi-sacred ground of several tribal elders, submitted a plan for moving the law school off campus to a building in the heart of the downtown area. The new law school should include a free legal clinic for the poor and indigent, he suggested.

The building could be renovated and remodeled without massive expenditures. It was near other downtown legal offices, as well as several government court buildings. It would provide a quick solution to the law school's overcrowded situation, he proposed.

Unfortunately for the dean, several of the tribal elders had been actively engaged in extended fund-raising efforts, and there, on page seventeen of an attractive brochure, was a beautiful watercolor rendering of the new on-campus law building.

The new dean's proposal clearly undermined their efforts and long range plans. The tribal elders, the fund raisers and gift givers, were men who had often regarded the downtown area as poor, dirty and undesirable.

The board decided to call in an outsider, a man-of-knowledge. They turned to a well known consulting firm, and the assignment filtered down to me.

I couldn't help but like the young law school dean. He was eager, ambitious, articulate. He explained the historical models of law school learning to me. He shared with me his concerns about insulating students from reality with ivy-covered walls.

"The law library would be here," he explained, as we reviewed a floor plan of the downtown building. "Classrooms in this section. We could even put in a student cafeteria at very low cost here," he pointed. "We would be very near the county and federal court buildings."

He had been so efficient. When his proposal was submitted he had already discussed the sale of the building with its owners. And he had obtained estimates for renovation and remodeling.

Still, the tone of the dean's voice suggested that he already knew he would lose. The consulting study was designed to find out how many other law schools had downtown or off-campus locations, and the dean already knew the answer. His proposal was innovative, and when the board found out how innovative they would be worried.

When the board of directors met to discuss the study results, the university pecking order remained in place. The dean lost his challenge. His proposal to relocate the law school off campus was voted down by the council of elders.

So the young dean joined the army of young tribesmen all over the world who get pushed and pulled by those above them. This time he had lost, but the process of tangling with the council of elders helped him identify the pecking order, the key personalities in the constellation of power and influence. He had been naive. He had not realized he was working in a tribe, that he was a new tribesman, and that success and advancement in the tribe depended a great deal on the discretion and support of the core group of chiefs and elders. Maybe next time he'd be more like the successful baboon in Goodall's story, sizing up the power structure before acting.

★   ★   ★

For human tribes, the most reliable method for defining the pecking order is to understand how food, property, possessions and wealth are divided.

The tribesman's position in the pecking order determines his compensation. This compensation takes many forms. Among the Sioux Indians the most powerful chiefs had many ponies. For early tribes it was a share of meat from the hunt. Early reports of cannibal tribes in New Guinea indicated that the best parts of their victims, the fingers and heart, were saved for the chief. Among the Kurelu tribes of New Guinea, wealth is pigs, and the man who can throw the biggest pig feast gains prestige, recognition and authority in the eyes of other tribesmen.

Wives and concubines were an indication of wealth in some biblical tribes. In certain African agricultural tribes the chief has the largest grain-storage bins. Malinowski[19] reported that the chief in certain Trobriand Island tribes had the largest yam-storage house. Yams, like base salary or stock options, were a reflection of position in the pecking order. At harvest time, tribesmen had to be careful that their pile of yams was not larger than that of the chief.

In modern business corporations, salaries, bonuses, and stock options provide the most precise definition of the pecking order. Titles help, but they are less accurate than compensation. Club memberships, free parking, expense accounts, and company cars tell the real story. Office space, location and furnishings are also provided according to the pecking order.

In government organizations, including universities where earnings are controlled by civil-service schedules, other methods are used to maintain a clear definition of the pecking order. Things like class assignments and committee memberships take on critical importance.

The top position in the pecking order of the corporate tribe gets the largest salary, the largest bonus and the largest number of stock option shares. It is significant that one of the main duties of the board of directors is the approval of salary increases, bonus and stock option awards for the top corporate positions.

Money is the symbol of position in the pecking order, and the amount an individual receives is correlated with his ascendancy or slippage in the pecking order. If an executive becomes aware that his bonus is smaller than that of other tribesmen whom he regards as peers, he may leave the tribe in anger or disappointment. The amount of bonus has far less meaning to him than his advancement or slippage in the pecking order. One man receives a $5,000 bonus. He discovers that one of his peers received $5,100. The extra $100 has profound psychological meaning.

Because such comparisons have powerful impact, many corporations attempt to hide the information. They discourage employees from discussing salary or bonus awards. In fact, there is a well-recognized tradition among executives that makes discussion of salary, bonus awards and stock options taboo. This taboo helps the chief and his top team keep order among the troops.

Most large corporations have a tradition, from whence they do not know, of dividing their payroll and pay programs into separate pieces. If you ask why, they'll probably say, "I don't know; that's the way we've always done it."

Hourly workers and those who are covered by union contracts represent one group. Then there are secretaries and clerical workers. Salaried workers, from college trainees to management, are a separate group. Executives like to have their payroll separate from the rest.

Those who share in the management bonus group represent another special group. The list of bonus recipients and awards is a highly confidential document—hot with significance. This "share of the hunt" document reveals changes in the pecking order. Some executives have moved ahead, some have slipped backward.

More powerful still is the list of stock-option holders and the records regarding the price of the stock when the option was granted. This is big medicine. Here, great fortunes are generated.

*   *   *

I was completing a long calculation. How much would (I shall call him) Fred Williams' stock options be worth if he held them until retirement? I had assumed the stock would continue its ten year 7% trend in appreciation. After capital gains, it came to $26 million!

I re-did my calculation—twice. It was correct.

They had given him $26 million! Had the compensation committee been aware of the potential value of their gift?

They wanted Fred to take over the presidency. They were sure he was the right man. To make the offer attractive, they had given him a stock option grant.

But Fred was a young man, ten years younger than any of the other option grantees. I was not sure if the full effect of compounding the growth over such a long time frame had been understood by the compensation committee. They had done it, in any case. If Fred could provide the continuing leadership they needed, he would become a very wealthy man.

*   *   *

Deep within the womb of the corporation, new capitalists are nurtured. Appreciating stock values give key top executives their first nipple, their first real opportunity to accumulate large amounts of capital.

Executives who receive the largest number of stock option shares also receive the largest salaries and bonus awards. And many who receive bonus awards are not high enough in the pecking order to be eligible for options.

Finally, there are the major stockholders, the owners and members of the board. ACME International's dividend was $3.00 a share in 1983. The chairman of the board, with 500,000 shares, received a check for $1,500,000.

Bloodless Battles

Few tribes have ever offered riches that can compare with those of modern business corporations, but unlike earlier tribes of men, corporations have amazingly little bloodshed associated with reshufflings of positions in the pecking order. Physical confrontations rarely occur. At every level in the corporate tribe some superior committee or individual has the last word. And even when stakes are extremely high there is no physical conflict. Feelings are hurt, to be sure. Careers are made or destroyed, but considering the stakes, it all happens with admirable smoothness.

I don't mean to describe corporations as polyanna perfect. Far from it. They are often ruthless in firings and layoffs. Left uncontrolled they will use as many resources as possible to grow at a maximum rate, sometimes at the expense of the environment and their own employees. So great is their appetite for survival and growth that laws must be passed and constantly enforced to assure that some of them do not cheat or mistreat their employees, pollute the environment or take unfair advantage of their competition.

But if the shedding of blood can be accepted as a simple benchmark of ethical behavior in human relationships, then the corporate tribe must be recognized as a significant improvement over earlier tribal adaptations. We see about us a clear reduction of bloodshed, of physical abuse and of slavery. Presidents are not executed by the board of directors. Employees are not sacrificed to the gods, tortured or killed. Corporate salesmen compete in the marketplace without bloodshed. New tribes grow and fail without resorting to armed combat. Shootings, stabbings or fist fights are rare within the corporate tribe. Corporal punishment is gone.

Some executives think their life is over when they get the ax. They suffer real pain. But most recover without serious long-term damage. They dust themselves off and are soon affiliated with a new tribe, often in a bigger job earning more money.

The Ubiquitous Pyramid

Take a group of men selected at random. Place this cluster on an island somewhere. Without fully realizing it, its members will begin to work out a pecking order. When they have finished, the resulting organization of relationships of dominance and subordinance, if diagrammed, will be pyramid shaped.

Pyramid-shaped organization structures may be a part of man's hereditary nature. They exist in modern business, in governmental agencies, hospitals, universities, professional organizations, armies, Elks Clubs, churches, prisons, charitable organizations—in short, wherever men are found in groups.

A few corporations have experimented with other organization forms. Abbott Laboratories in North Chicago, Control Data in Minneapolis, and some aerospace corporations, have experimented with "matrix" organizations. In fact, experiments with the multiple reporting relationships of matrix organization styles appeared to be a major trend in the late 1970s. But all these corporate tribes operated under the general umbrella of a pyramid-shaped top officer group. No one, to my knowledge, changed the hierarchy of their compensation programs or redesigned offices to eliminate size differences.

Likewise, a few attempts have been made to manage by committee, to operate with leaderless groups or to invert the triangle (encourage the lowest-level employees to formulate policy decisions, set wages, working hours, etc.). But the pyramid is so frequently observed—probably in 100% of the companies listed in Fortune's 500—that one is tempted to conclude that it is a result of deeply embedded tribal roots.

In his book, *The Yam Factor*[20], Martin Page indicated after studying the Akwaaba tribe of Ngonga, that:

> *"Modern corporations, although without realizing it, appear to have modelled their hierarchical structures on those of savage tribes. Furthermore, several offices generally believed to be peculiar to business organizations have proved on investigation to have the most primitive origins.*

While in Ngonga, we prepared with the help of palace officials an outline organization chart of the Akwaaba. It turned out like this:

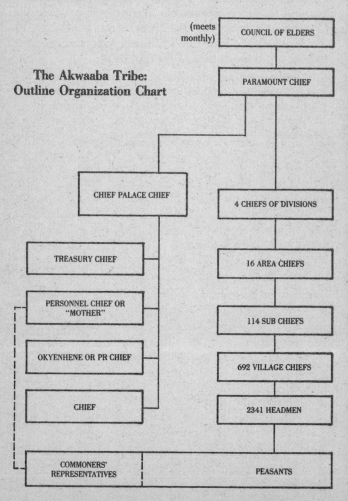

(meets monthly)

COUNCIL OF ELDERS

PARAMOUNT CHIEF

**The Akwaaba Tribe:
Outline Organization Chart**

CHIEF PALACE CHIEF

4 CHIEFS OF DIVISIONS

TREASURY CHIEF

16 AREA CHIEFS

PERSONNEL CHIEF OR "MOTHER"

114 SUB CHIEFS

OKYENHENE OR PR CHIEF

692 VILLAGE CHIEFS

CHIEF

2341 HEADMEN

COMMONERS' REPRESENTATIVES

PEASANTS

We found it interesting to compare this organization chart with that of an American corporation:

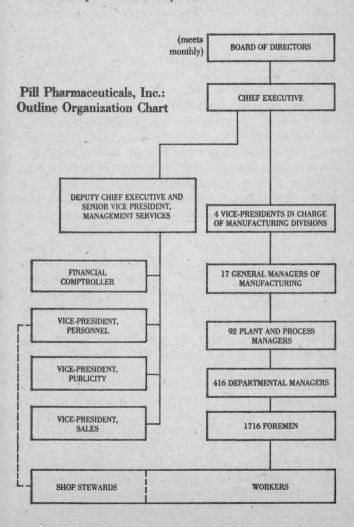

(meets monthly) BOARD OF DIRECTORS

Pill Pharmaceuticals, Inc.: Outline Organization Chart

CHIEF EXECUTIVE

DEPUTY CHIEF EXECUTIVE AND SENIOR VICE PRESIDENT, MANAGEMENT SERVICES

4 VICE-PRESIDENTS IN CHARGE OF MANUFACTURING DIVISIONS

FINANCIAL COMPTROLLER

17 GENERAL MANAGERS OF MANUFACTURING

VICE-PRESIDENT, PERSONNEL

92 PLANT AND PROCESS MANAGERS

VICE-PRESIDENT, PUBLICITY

416 DEPARTMENTAL MANAGERS

VICE-PRESIDENT, SALES

1716 FOREMEN

SHOP STEWARDS

WORKERS

Mr. Page may have pushed his comparison a bit, but the basic concept that modern corporations and so called "primitive" tribes organize in similar ways clearly supports the central thesis of this book.

Everywhere one looks, in American Indian tribes, in Africa, South America, in hunting-gathering tribes, seacoast fishing tribes, island tribes, pastoral tribes, as well as agricultural tribes, the pattern is there—an ancient template—a pyramid.

These elemental pyramids grew larger and more complex during the agricultural era. Moses led the multitudes of Israel, which were divided into twelve family-oriented tribes. These were further divided into pyramid-shaped family groups.

Our grandfathers, the last of the agricultural tribesmen, also formed small family-cluster pyramids to work their farms. Sons were a clear asset to a farmer, especially when they began to assume adult work responsibilities.

The families of the farming era spread themselves thinly over the crop-producing land, particularly in North America, Europe and Asia. The villages and towns, in particular the churches, provided central meeting places. Here the singing, marriages, baptisms, christenings and funerals occurred.

The council huts for our grandfathers were white. They had spires. They can be found in the heart of every farming community. These, together with town, city, county and state governments, were tribal headquarters. Each was ruled by a dominant male, by councils of elders, and a pyramid-shaped, pecking-ordered cluster of bonded males.

The pyramid emerges in all human groups. It is those groups which lack a hierarchy which are unstable. And they will remain unstable until nature takes its course and a new pecking order is in place.

The pyramid has been around for a long time. It is a basic building block of human organizations. Some organization theorists, chafing with the frustration of being buried somewhere on the lower rungs of the pecking order, like to throw rocks at the pyramid. Eager to innovate and appear erudite, they recommend new organization forms. Some corporations have tried variations. But they all come back. The president stays at the top. The key line and staff sub-chiefs remain in place. Fanned out below them are pyramid-shaped organization structures.

An insatiable appetite for acquisitions during the 60s resulted in hundreds of strange new conglomerated corporations, pyramids on top of pyramids, hierarchies of profit centers with dissimilar product lines. Everybody got into the act. Railroads, insurance companies, even banks, formed holding companies to permit diversification.

Prior to conglomerates, corporations which stuck to the traditional, functional type organization (sales, production, finance, etc.), were also made up of pyramids within pyramids. Each department head was the leader of a pyramid.

Whether the subchiefs of a corporate tribe are department heads or subsidiary presidents, they all provide leadership for pyramid-shaped operating units.

Organization psychologists point out that each individual in the corporation who has supervision responsibility is a connecting point. He is at the top of one pyramid and somewhere below the top of another pyramid—the one his boss commands. He is a linking pin. His goals and objectives also fit into an interlocking pyramid design. As a department head or work group leader, a manager's personal objectives are the same as the group targets for those who report to him. But his personal objectives represent only a chunk of his boss's goals.

The Association of Humanist Psychologists (AHP), held a convention in New Orleans in 1974. I attended primarily to hear Stanley Krippner report on his studies of healing arts and shaman of tribes in Brazil and the Philippines.

★   ★   ★

The AHP convention is a mind-blowing experience. There are primal screamers screaming, conventioners hugging and kissing in the lobby, elevator, bar, pool, coffee shop and men's room. There are Gestaltists and feminists, go-nude advocates, biofeedbackers, acupuncturists, meditators, flower children and a few organization development psychologists. I was among the latter.

I noticed on the program a session with a title something like "The AHP, A Look at Our Organization." The AHP is supposed to be dedicated to maximum freedom and individual enrichment for everyone. In several meetings, those in attendance seemed to agree that corporations were giant freedom gobblers, stripping people of their dignity. So I was curious to see how the AHP was organized. How had an organization with such humanistic ideals organized itself to serve its members?

I had hoped for a round table, at least, but was not too surprised to find that the AHP's organization was pyramid shaped. It had a council of elders. Its officers rotated through the chairs like so many other associations.

★   ★   ★

The pyramid is here to stay. Executives should take it as a given. Accept it. Learn about it. The experience of living within these pyramids is something corporate executives share with tribesmen everywhere. We all have known dominant males, chiefs, fellow tribesmen. We share these experiences with every link, every generation of men from farmers and hunters back among the twigs and branches of evolution's tree, right down to the human roots of six million or more years ago.

Our Tribal Regalia

An anthropologist sent by some advanced civilization may describe a corporate executive in ways that would surprise us.

One can picture the scientist taking notes as he observes a corporate tribesman prepare for a day at the office:

* * *

Washes body with heated water piped into his hut.

Scrapes hair carefully from cheeks, chin and neck with sharpened hand tool.

Rubs perfumed substance into armpits to prevent perspiration, which is regarded as taboo.

Carefully arranges hair with another special hand tool.

Selects costume for the day. Munsingwear loin cloth, several layers of cloth coverings over torso, arms and legs. These are kept free of wrinkles with metal heat machines. Leather shoes or boots (polished with a special wax), a leather strap or cinch about the waist, various pieces of ornamentation, a colorful sash or ribbon knotted about the neck and left hanging to the waist, and finally, a small machine, strapped to the wrist, which hums or ticks softly.

The costumes vary in color, within limits, particularly the ribbon worn about the neck. Most of the coverings are bland or dark shades of brown, blue or grey. Females display more brilliant colors.

Tribes are led by adult males. These tribes are located in large vertical hive-like villages made up of smaller cubicles connected by passageways. The more important the chief, the larger is his cubicle.

Like other tribes, members are organized in pyramid-shaped pecking orders. Each chief is attended by subchiefs, who in turn are attended by various subordinate tribesmen and women. The pecking order is maintained by a complex series of titles and privileges, as well as through a periodic division of tribal earnings.

* * *

How perplexed anthropologists will be, in a million years, to discover that in the midst of our technological achievements many of our modern offices, headquarters of the corporate tribes, have no 13th floor.

On a Certain Blindness In Corporate Tribesmen

In many ways, far more ways than we realize, behavior in the modern corporation is governed by ancient rules. Yet, we are largely blind to them. They seem so normal and ordinary to us that we fail to recognize them for what they are. Shaking hands as a greeting ritual is no more sensible than bowing, hugging, rubbing noses, kissing cheeks or slapping one another on the chest or back, as was the Tierra del Fuegan's custom. Yet, to us the handshake greeting seems normal and ordinary.

We are, in ways, as driven by irrational fears and superstitions as those who preceded us. We suffer the same egocentrism that caused the elders to burn Copernicus at the stake for daring to suggest that the earth was not the center of the universe. We love to see ourselves as the center of the universe, above the animals, far more civilized than so-called primitive cultures. We're special, chosen, intelligent, god-like creatures. To accept that we may still be a bit primitive is demeaning. Our natural reaction when observing cultures different from our own is to assume that our way is better, more logical, morally superior.

Many of us, because of our desire for being significant, tend to accept a time warp in our view of history. We tend to judge all history by our own 75-year slice of it, and to think of our own age as most significant.

Our appreciation of the elapsed time of, say, the stone age, also becomes distorted. It shrinks. We fail to appreciate or comprehend the length of a million years, or how paltry and insignificant is the tiny slice of time that is our life span. This time warp shrinks the significance and importance of previous ages. It leads us to believe we have progressed far beyond our primitive beginnings.

The readers of *National Geographic* are entranced by the strange appearances, ceremonies, customs and taboos of jungle tribes. Yet we are blind to parallels in our own situations. The modern observer cringes at photographs and descriptions of African circumcision ceremonies, all the time forgetting that nestled in his own Munsingwear loin cloth is a circumcised penis.

Of course, if challenged he will provide a lengthy dissertation about the logic and sensibleness of his own circumcision practices. But the roots of this ceremony are ancient, at least as old as the Old Testament, probably much older. To be sure, our rationalizations have become more sophisticated, but the ritual has remained relatively unchanged for ages.

Some Basic Tribal Principles

Corporations are the latest leaves on the branch of evolving human groups. In many basic ways, corporations still retain the unmistakable stamp of their tribal origins.

- Within both corporations and tribes, both men and women form working clusters. Anthropologists refer to this tendency as "male and female bonding."

- Both corporations and tribes are organized into dominance hierarchies. This yields pyramid-shaped organization structures.

- These pyramid-shaped clusters are the basic building blocks of both tribes and corporations. Large groups of workers are made up of several levels of interlocked pyramids, each with its own dominant person, pecking order, competitive struggles, and operating traditions.

- Alpha—the king, chief, president, or in some cases the queen—the dominant person at the top of the pyramid, is found in animal groups, tribes and corporations.

- Both corporations and tribes function with review and guidance from one or more councils of elders.

- Both tribes and corporations avail themselves of advice and direction from "men and women of knowledge". The terms "headshrinker, high-powered attorney, financial wizard, fetisher, brujo, bara'u, sorcerer, consultant, shaman, witch doctor, medicine man, prophet, and priest," as well as "sorceress, witch, priestess, and prophetess," all refer to archetypal roles common to tribes, modern and primitive, past and present, throughout the world.

- Both corporations and tribes divide property according to the pecking order. The symbol of wealth changes. It can be wives, ponies, grain bins, yams, gold or stock options, but the dominant person—usually a male—gets the most, followed by his key subchiefs, and so forth.

- Both abide by territorial rules within their organizations. Whether it is a central hut, palace, head table or a corner office with a view, the leaders occupy prime bits of territory.

- Both corporations and tribes identify and operate within defined territories.

- Both corporations and tribes have the same ultimate objectives. They are survival and growth.

To recognize our primitive roots and become aware of the ways they influence our corporate behavior may be of critical importance.

The knowledge may help us to face up to reality, to accept corporations as a fact of life, as essential to the survival and growth of our species. Rather than kick against them we should get on with the task of making them better, more fulfilling places to spend our prime adult years.

Chapter Two

❧

TRIBAL TERRITORY

My oldest friend is a semi-eccentric scientist. He has always had an interest in animals and their habits. In college he usually had an odd assortment of rodents wandering about his apartment. Once during an intense philosophical argument, I was surprised to notice a guinea pig suddenly peek out at me from under his armchair. My first thought was that the animal kingdom was obviously on his side. On another occasion he introduced me to a family of laboratory mice which he was raising in his bathtub.

He gave me a fascinating demonstration. The rodents he kept about him had divided his apartment into territories. White mice controlled the kitchen. A larger gray mouse controlled the living room area. The boundary line was a strip of aluminum in a doorway which separated the carpet from the kitchen linoleum.

First my friend put the dominant white mouse about six feet into the living room. Like lightning, he was attacked by the wild gray bully. No contest. The white mouse shot back into the kitchen like a streak. The gray mouse stopped the chase abruptly at the aluminum strip.

My friend explained the boundary lines. Then he lifted the large gray bully by the tail and dropped it about six feet into the kitchen. This time the smaller white mouse attacked as the gray scrambled for traction on the slick floor. The home court advantage clearly outweighed obvious size and weight differences. This time the larger gray mouse was running like mad to escape.

I didn't realize it at the time, but I was observing a principle of nature that has profound implications. Robert Ardrey covers the principle eloquently in *The Territorial Imperative*.[19] His book created an awakening to the importance of territory in understanding animal and human behavior.

Fish, birds and animals, including man, all exhibit various forms of territorial behavior. For many species the capture and defense of territory is an unrelenting, life-long struggle. Male bears, otters, dogs and lions mark territorial boundaries with feces or urine.

While walking my beagle past a neighbor's home I noted that he growled and the hair on his back raised after he sniffed a tree base. He also turned to look at the neighbor's house when he caught the collie's scent. Then, keeping a close watch, he urinated on the tree base—and went through a ritual ground pawing to cover competing scents. Male dogs never seem to tire of the life-long task of sniffing for territorial markers and depositing their own claims.

Every morning male birds of all kinds announce control of their hunting territories by flying to a high branch and singing, crowing, chirping, screaming their Tarzan scream.

Among mammals, securing and defense of territory is ordinarily a masculine behavior. Female lions hunt. Male lions, like male dogs, mark their territory with urine and attempt to drive off other males. Male bears mark their territories with feces and by reaching high to tear off a patch of tree bark. The larger the bear, the higher and larger the patch.

Man is clearly a territorial beast. He displaces animals that compete with him for territorial dominance. In defense of his home turf he can be an imposing adversary. On someone else's territory he is ill at ease, a guest or intruder, uncomfortable. If he is a burglar, he is ready to run. On his own turf he is far more confident and far more difficult to displace.

Men have filled libraries with documents of legal battles over real estate. Thousands of wars have been waged to capture or defend territory.

We divide territory by nations, states, counties, sections, blocks, plots, acres and yards. Within our hierarchies, we have specialists who measure, with precision, the boundaries of our property. Office space, like the size of one's yard and house, expresses man's deep and abiding concern over territory.

Changes in Food-getting Knowledge

If an alien space ship had been monitoring the surface of the earth with a great camera for thousands of years, its inhabitants would, in the last 100 years, have noted a strange phenomenon. Geometric, crystal-like structures would have been seen to grow here and there where human populations were dense. From space, the new skyscrapers of the corporate tribes in cities all over the world would have made the earth's surface look very different than it had for so many millions of years, especially at night when all the lights are blazing.

A cross section of these new tribal structures would show them to be honeycombed. Side-by-side, on top and bottom, they are made up of rectangular boxes connected by hallways and elevators. They are hive-like. They rise like giant termite hills.

Our alien space camera would have recorded another amazing change in the surface appearance of the earth, beginning about 10,000 years ago. As the forests were cleared and the fields of agriculturalists began to spread, the familiar patchwork pattern of plowed fields began to decorate the earth's surface. In North and South America most of this dramatic change occurred only in the past 200 years.

In the multi-million-year history of Homo-sapiens there have been two major changes in man's fundamental relationships to his food-provider territory. Both occurred as a result of refinements in food-getting knowledge.

The first change was from hunting and gathering to agriculture. It began about 10,000 years ago.

The second change was from agriculture to industry. It began about 100 years ago.

By studying some of the profound changes in man that resulted from the first territorial adaptation, we may be able to better understand the second, more recent one.

The Happy Hunting Ground

For man, territory is the source of food. Within early man's food-provider territory—his hunting grounds—he was both a predator and a harvester of roots, fruit, nuts, berries and insects. Both his bivouac and his food-providing territories were staked out by natural geographical features of the environment, such as mountains, rivers and oceans, which provided boundaries and protection.

The hunting territory was larger, more flexible, more difficult to defend, and less stoutly defended than the tribal compound. A given patch of hunting territory might be exploited by several tribes. On the other hand, because protection of the young and pregnant females was essential to survival, the tribal compound was both hidden and vigorously defended.

For many hunting-gathering tribes, the village was frequently moved, but sites for establishing camps were carefully selected as defendable, and often re-used. Many tribes moved seasonally. Because they moved frequently, they built temporary shelters. They had few belongings, only items which could be carried. The boundaries of nomadic tribes' hunting and food-gathering territories were well known to the tribesmen.

No one knows how many million years it took for hunter-gatherers to spread out over the entire surface of the earth, but hunting-gathering tribes have existed almost everywhere. One might speculate that as long as the supply of game and virgin hunting grounds were available, conflicts to capture or control territory were less urgent.

As the density of hunter-gatherers increased world-wide, the laws of supply and demand undoubtedly increased the frequency of territorial conflicts. Prime hunting grounds, like prime cropland, provided ample incentive for territorial warfare.

At the borders of their territory, hunting-gathering tribes maintained relationships with neighboring tribes that fluctuated between alliance and enmity. And the roles of adult males shifted frequently between hunting and war.

It is clear that primitive men and women survived by virtue of an intimate relationship to their food-providing territory. They developed in-depth knowledge of plants and animals, as well as the skills required for survival. These skills varied according to the climate, geography and indigenous food supplies.

The seal-hunting skills of the Eskimo were passed from one generation to the next, and were both essential for survival and unique to their arctic climate. When Australian aborigines spot an animal trail they gradually move brush and sticks to create natural barriers along the edge. Patiently, a little each day, they form a wall to guide and direct the animals. Finally, they prepare a trap. Similar keys of tribal wisdom, unique to a given environment, were essential for all hunting-gathering tribes.

Primitive man's relationship to his provider territory was probably delicate. In the 1880s, Stanley[23] reported that many of the African tribesmen who became displaced from their homelands by a few hundred miles, as a result of joining his expedition, became listless, sickly and died.

Human tribes, like various animal species, wax and wane. Those which master their territory become more numerous. Those which do not adapt to changing conditions first dwindle in size, and eventually become extinct.

Often, the changes in territorial conditions which result in extinction are subtle events; slight alterations in food supply, customs, or traditions, that gather momentum as they take hold and unravel.

The Tiano Indians that met Columbus 491 years ago no longer exist. Columbus, a representative of an agricultural nation-state, was the first hint of a radical change that would eventually lead the Tianos to extinction.

Samuel Eliot Morison's essay on the discovery of America includes these translations from Columbus's logs and correspondence:[24]

> "*Saturday, October 13: At daybreak there came to the beach many of these men, all young men as I have said and all of good stature, very handsome people. Their hair is not kinky but loose and coarse like horsehair; and the whole forehead and head is very broad, more so than any other race that I have seen, and the eyes very handsome and not small, and themselves not at all black, but of the color of the Canary Islanders . . . Their legs are very straight, all in a line; and no belly, but very well built. They came to the ship in dugouts which are fashioned like a long boat from the whole of a tree, and all in one piece, and wonderfully made (considering the country), and so big that in some came 40 to 50 men, and others smaller, down to the size that held but a single man. They row with a thing like a baker's peel and go wonderfully (fast), and if they capsize all begin to swim and right it and bail it out with calabashes that they carry. They brought skeins of spun cotton, and parrots and darts and other trifles that would be tedious to describe, and gave all for whatever was given to them.*
>
> "*They are so ingenuous and free with all they have, that no one would believe it who has not seen it; of anything that they possess, if it be asked of them, they never say no; on the contrary, they invite you to share it and show as much love as if their hearts went with it, and they are content with whatever trifle be given them, whether it be a thing of value or of petty worth. I forbade that they be given things so*

worthless as bits of broken crockery and of green glass and lacepoints, although when they could get them, they thought they had the best jewel in the world."

Morison tells us that the Tianos had controlled their island territories for about 100 years prior to Columbus's arrival. Emigrating from South America, they had conquered or enslaved the previous, more primitive inhabitants known as the Sibony. The Tianos were a relatively advanced people. They grew corn, yams and roots, made bread, pottery and shell utensils. Their only weapon was a short spear or dart. Columbus noted the tribe's vulnerability. On the same day he discovered the people, he recognized how easily they could be enslaved. Two days later, he made this entry:[25]

"October 14: These people are very unskilled in arms . . . with fifty men they could all be subjected and made to do all that one wished."

The Tianos were conquered and enslaved. But they did not adapt to these radical changes in their simple existence. After they were moved from their villages to plantations, their white masters complained that they were unfit for hard work. They became listless and depressed, could not eat. Unable to adapt, they died by the hundreds.

An Old, Familiar Story

This story is a very old one, one that has been replayed thousands of times in the several million years of man's history. And the process is still going on, full blast. The Narranganset Indians, a proud American Indian tribe several short generations ago, are now extinct. So are the Potomacs, the Pequots, the Mohicans, the Pokonoket, the Wampanoags, the Chesapeakes and the Chicahominys. There were an estimated 3,000 Yahgan Indians in Tierra del Fuego on the southern tip of South America when Darwin stopped there in 1832, while on his famous cruise aboard the H.M.S. Beagle. In 1973, only two remained. The Tasmanian Indians discovered by Captain Cook were all gone by 1898. The Hawaiian race is almost gone, decimated by epidemics and disease imported by early white men.

Claude Levi–Strauss[26] indicates that early agricultural settlers in Brazil actually hung garments of recent smallpox victims, together with trinkets and bells, along trails frequented by Indians.

Disease appears to have been a frequent result when primitive people come into contact with foreigners. It also occurred when hunter-gatherers were detached from their ancestral food-providing territory. American Indian tribes which were moved a few hundred miles to reservations on unfamiliar territory, died by the hundreds from dysentery, epidemics and diseases.

When the Poncas were forced to move from their ancestral home in the Dakotas to a reservation in Arkansas, they died rapidly. By the end of the first year on the new reservation, one-fourth of the tribe had died. Their chief, White Eagle, watched them dwindle. *"The land was good, but in the summer we were sick again. We were as grass that is trodden down; we and our stock. Then came the cold weather, and how many died we did not know."*[27]

More recently, the Hadza tribe of the remote bush country of Africa were forced to relocate to a reservation only 50 miles from their ancestral homeland. They had been a successful hunting-gathering tribe, living in beehive-shaped grass huts, having an abundant food supply and a relatively large amount of leisure time. A visiting pediatrician from Makerere University indicated that the Hadza children were among the healthiest in East Africa. In the first year after their move, an epidemic claimed one-fourth of the children.

Sometimes subtle changes which bring about initial survival advantages spell doom over the long run.

The horse was introduced to American Indian culture via Spanish explorers in the late 1700s. Before that, the Cheyenne had been a relatively sedentary people who lived in earth-lodge villages along tributaries of the Missouri River. The horse changed the Cheyenne completely. Horses revolutionized buffalo hunting, and the Cheyenne adapted quickly to a life of near total dependence on the buffalo for food, clothes and shelter.

Buffalo scattered during the part of the year when grazing was poor, and gathered in the summer mating season when grass was lush enough to support the united herd. The Cheyenne followed them. They too, divided into family-grouped hunting bands which joined together in the summer for tribal ceremonies and a communal hunt.

The Cheyenne became active competitors for hunting territory, engaging in border skirmishes and raids for horses. The skills required for leadership emphasized courage in war, riding skill and marksmanship, and young men had to continually prove their capabilities in these areas.

The Cheyenne evolved rapidly. Within 150 years they had become flexible, semi-nomadic, fast-reacting buffalo hunters.

But heavy dependence on the buffalo for subsistence emerged as a critical source of vulnerability to the Cheyenne when an extended drought, and the slaughter of herds took place in the 1850s. The evolving environment of the Cheyenne—first the horse, then the buffalo, and finally the increasing encroachment of white men—threatened the tribe's survival.

Hunting-gathering tribes have been disappearing for the past 10,000 years. Their decline is in inverse proportion to the growth of agricultural tribes. In North America, the happy hunting grounds where buffalo roamed evolved into cropland in fewer than 100 years.

A dwindling number of hunting-gathering tribes still exist. In his book *People of the Lake*,[28] Richard Leakey estimates the current world-wide population of hunter-gatherers to be only 300,000. Exposure to technology appears to speed the rate of their extinction.

Although a few tribes in the African and South American jungles still control their own territories, most current hunting-gathering tribes are only allowed to exist (some are even protected), by modern governments which no longer regard them as serious competitors for territory.

The Transition to Agriculture

We have a dim record of the impact of agriculture in the ancient Egyptian myth of Osiris:[29]

> *"Reigning as king on earth, Osiris reclaimed the Egyptians from savagery, gave them laws, and taught them to worship the gods. Isis, the sister and wife of Osiris, discovered wheat and barley growing wild, and Osiris introduced the cultivation of these grains amongst his people, who forthwith abandoned cannibalism and took kindly to a corn diet. Moreover, Osiris is said to have been the first to gather fruit from trees, to train the vine to poles, and to tread the grapes. Eager to communicate these beneficent discoveries to all mankind, he committed the whole government of Egypt to his wife Isis, and travelled over the world, diffusing the blessings of civilization and agriculture wherever he went ... Loaded with the wealth that had been showered upon him by grateful nations, he returned to Egypt, and on account of the benefits he had conferred on mankind he was unanimously hailed and worshipped as a deity."*

Here was a person who could grow food, seen as a god by the hungry and more primitive hunter-gatherers in Egypt.

Kilton Stewart traveled back and forth between hunting-gathering and agricultural tribes during his field work in the Philippines. In his book *Pygmies and Dream Giants*,[30] he describes the Negrito, still essentially hunters and gatherers; the Ilongot, who had learned to till the land and build more permanent shelters; and the Ifugao, who were deeply entrenched in rice farming.

The Ifugao believed in a major god, Lindum, the Giver. "He gave the Ifugao their domesticated animals, their technology, and their ritual."

In contrast, the Negritos worshipped animal gods. They "participated in wild, half-prayerful, half-magical dances, expressing thanksgiving to the animals which had allowed themselves to be found and killed for food . . ."

When man discovered how to grow his food, his view of the universe changed. New gods and goddesses of fertility emerged with agriculture. Corn gods, yam gods, rice gods, grain gods, rain gods and sun gods. The first organized religions and large community worship houses emerged.

Man's tribal structure also changed. Now that he had to tend his crop, he stopped being nomadic and built more permanent structures. The first cities emerged, and with them the first armies. Territorial boundaries grew into nation-states. Complex religious and government institutions emerged for the first time. Man evolved from a hunter to a farmer—from a warrior to a soldier.

As long as men used a territory for hunting or food gathering, the only notion of private ownership was that related to one's hut and possessions.

In frontier America, Indian negotiators kept trying to convince the white, European, agriculturally oriented peoples that no one owned the hunting grounds. They belonged to everyone. However, Indians did maintain and defend tribal hunting territory and conducted raids into the territories of other tribes. Encroachment by other tribes was resisted as a cooperative effort by the adult males.

At the root of it all, the transition from hunting-gathering to agriculture may be one result of man's finally understanding the "facts of life." He probably lacked this knowledge for the first several millions of years of his existence. The fact that many hunting-gathering tribes were matriarchal (traced their lineage and tribal affiliations through their mothers) suggests that earlier men were unaware of their role in conception. There were no fathers in these early tribes.

When this germ of information, so long in coming to light, finally took hold, it may have planted the seeds of agriculture. The knowledge required for the growing of crops and the breeding of animals may have been a prerequisite for the change from matriarchal to patriarchal tracing of lineage. Womankind must have lost both power and influence when men finally discovered their role in producing new tribespeople.

The farmer feels differently about territory than the hunter-gatherer. The age of agriculture has been an age of armies and wars to capture, own, and control crop-producing land. Earlier tribes had skirmishes for hunting territory, but armies were a new dimension—different in scale from anything that had previously existed.

The 10,000-year era of agriculture represents an extremely bloody chapter in man's evolution. The strong continued to destroy the weak. Ranks and files of warriors continually killed and died to protect furrows and rows of crops. The blood of the soldier nourished the crop land he conquered and defended. Mass slaughter of soldiers from defeated tribes was common.

Old Testament Testimony

As an anthropological document, the Old Testament is essentially the history of an early agricultural tribe. When the tribe of Israel defeated the Midianites, all the adult men were put to the sword. Then all the male children were slaughtered. Then all the women who were not virgins were killed. The Bible does not give a head count of the thousands that were slaughtered, but it does tell us how many virgins were spared—there were thirty-two thousand![32]

Where men continued the hunting-gathering life in pursuit of wild food, political structures remained relatively simple.

At first agriculture merely supplemented the diet of the hunting-gathering tribes, and in some areas of the world this pattern persists. Certain nomadic South American tribes that move with the seasons merely harvest crops that were planted during a previous occupation of that territory. In other areas, where the soil is too weak to sustain several successive growing seasons, the nomadic pattern and slash-and-burn farming techniques still persist.

When men began to till the land and their villages became more permanent, the complexity of the political and religious structures dramatically increased. Agriculture preceded and was a necessary prerequisite for permanent villages and complex governmental structures, including armies. Those who argue that war is inevitable should realize that organized horde warfare, as we know it, emerged rather recently, with agriculture, about 10,000 years ago.

A nation or a state, simply stated, is a patch of territory. William the Conqueror divided a conquered kingdom into 60,000 parcels of land, each nearly equal in value. From each, the service of one soldier was due. Land ownership was the source of armies, and control of land meant power.

In ancient Egypt, every soldier was a landowner with an allotment of about six acres. In Greece, the conquering Hellenes rewarded each soldier with an endowment of land. In Rome, each landowner was under obligation to serve in the military; and in ancient England, a man could lose his hereditary land ownership by misconduct in battle.

The broad evolutionary change that turned man from a hunter-gatherer to a farmer seems to follow similar progressions on different continents.

Hawaii, because of its isolation from European influence before Captain Cook in 1768, and because of its relatively advanced agricultural civilization, provides some fascinating parallels to other agricultural civilizations. In *On the Hana Coast*, Ron Youngblood[32] describes how Hawaii's increasing population of agriculturalists divided the available land.

> *"As the population began to increase, a few centuries after the initial settlement, the presence of people began to have an impact on the 'āina, the land. By 1200 A.D. the more marginal lands were permanently settled, and by 1400 A.D. forests were replaced by cultivated fields and valley basins were converted to vast irrigation systems.*
>
> *"The increasing population also led to greater social complexity, and a feudal system of land management evolved,*

> *with each island headed by at least one mōʻī, or king. The best lands were reserved for the king. The rest were allotted to warrior chiefs who, in turn, gave direct control of some lands to their most faithful followers, and so on, with the divisions of land becoming smaller and the lowest portion going to the common people."*

Unfortunately, the tribal warfare in isolated Hawaii, just as in Europe, China, and Africa, was a major and continuous adult male activity. And just as in Old Testament accounts of an earlier agricultural people, the consequences of losing a territorial battle were severe. Fornander's account of the seige of Ka-ʻuiki, in about 1780, shows how the losing chiefs and their soldiers were treated following a major battle.[33]

> *"The Hawaii chiefs were well provisioned and the fort held out stoutly until Kahekili was advised to cut off the water supply of the fort by damming and diverting the springs in the neighborhood. The measure succeeded, and the garrison, making desperate sorties beyond their lines to procure water, were slain in numbers and finally surrendered, expecting no mercy and obtaining none . . . large numbers of Hawaii chiefs and soldiers were slain and their corpses burnt at Kuawalu and at Honuaula (heiau)."*

Territory, or land, also provided the basis for taxes, tributes and the wealth accumulated by governing bodies.

The territorial holdings of agriculturally based tribes served to amplify the stratification of social classes. In ancient Japan and India soldiers formed a separate hereditary class, supported completely by a farmer class. The landowners were a privileged class, separate from soldiers and farmers. Slave classes were composed of people who had been separated from their territory by conquest. Hunter-gatherers also had slaves, usually women or children captured in raids on other tribes. Ordinarily, they were gradually absorbed into the mainstream of tribal life.

As agricultural tribes generated food surpluses, trade increased. Complex economic systems evolved among tribes as they mastered the skill of growing food and domesticating animals. An in-depth analysis of specific phases and steps in the emergence of classes, craftsmen, and guilds is beyond the scope of this book. Engles' classical analysis, *"The Origin of the Family, Private Property and the State"*[34], first published in 1884, will be a useful reference for interested readers.

Agricultural tribes emerged wherever men came in contact with grain-bearing grasses in the broad bands of flood plains which spread out from forest and mountain areas, especially in temperate zones. The pushing aside of hunting-gathering tribes by those who grew their food occurred in a domino-like chain reaction all over the world. Wherever men came into contact with fertile cropland, the hunters and gatherers were pushed aside, killed, conquered and enslaved by farmer-soldiers.

Raising crops resulted in new patterns of distribution of people across the land. Whereas highly mobile adult male hunting bands dispersed to cover areas for hunting game during the day, and re-formed with females, elders and children into larger tribal clusters in the evenings, agriculturists spread themselves more thinly and in smaller family clusters across the crop-producing territory, especially in the broad grasslands of the temperate zones in Europe, Asia, and the Americas. The break-up of matriarchal tribal clusters into father-mother-children family units may have been one of the most significant results of the transition from hunting and gathering to agriculture. Permanent dwellings were built in the fields. Nightly tribal gatherings evolved into less frequent weekend gatherings in centralized villages.

Both the houses in the fields and the villages became more permanent. The emergence of walled cities, fortresses and castles corresponded to a stage in the evolution of agricultural civilizations when armies constantly struggled to dominate and control surrounding cropland. When security of the tribe was threatened, the farmers retreated into these centralized forts and walled cities for defense.

The age of agriculture was also an age of organized religions. Wars for control of the cropland were usually holy wars for domination of one belief system over another. Terms such as infidel, heretic, barbarians, and heathens were used by various church-states to define the enemy. Armies were sanctioned by the hometown god, and the millions of farmer-soldiers who struggled to expand or defend their cropland usually believed God was on their side, and the enemy was corrupted by some evil religion.

Our grandfather farmers owned, controlled or worked patches of food-provider territory. They actively competed for cropland. At church, on weekends, they participated in tribal ceremonies. Our grandfathers' tribal villages contained market areas and the ceremonial hut (white with a spire and a bell). They were located in the center of surrounding croplands. As with hunting territory, the cropland was defended as a community effort.

The Emergence of Corporate Tribes

Within the last 100 years, the cropland has become sparsely populated. Like huge magnets, emerging corporations have drawn the population off the cropland to the offices and factories of the cities. This, too, represents a fundamental change in man's basic relationship to territory.

Corporations are as significant in altering and modifying man's basic relationship to territory as was agriculture. Most corporations have come into being in the past 100 years. The most dramatic growth has been in the past 50 years. They are blossoming in logarithmic progressions all over the world.

Visualize this 100-year tidbit of time in man's anthropological time frame of 6 million years (a conservative estimate, in view of recent 14,000,000-year-old archeological findings).

Take a tape measure. Let 100 years equal one inch. Nail one end of the tape measure to the floor and mark off 6 million years. You will find that you must pace over 16½ football fields laid end to end.

The momentum of human evolution was already rolling 16½ football fields ago. About 3 yards ago, men discovered agriculture. They stopped wandering. Stable villages emerged, as well as the first cities, armies, governments and churches.

About one yard ago the Old Testament was written. Just under 20 inches ago Christ was crucified.

One inch ago, corporations emerged! As much as we might like to forget our tribal origins, we cannot escape or disassociate ourselves from the momentum of millions of years of steady evolutionary development.

In the context of the multi-million year time frame of anthropology, the birth of corporate tribes appears as a dramatic burst of economic growth. It ripples through nation after nation.

W.W. Rostow[35] traces the takeoff in Britain, France, Germany, Russia, Japan, China, Turkey, Mexico and the United States. All revealed sudden bursts of economic growth associated with the emergence of new primary industries.

Just as agricultural tribes swept the hunter-gatherers from all the tillable land in a domino-like chain reaction throughout the world, so also have corporations been sweeping through the world, drawing men off the cropland into the cities.

Just as the missionaries, explorers, and other representatives of agricultural civilizations penetrated into the most primitive nooks and crannies of the earth, introducing new customs, religions, and traditions, so also are the representatives of the corporate tribes, the salesmen, engineers, accountants, attorneys and consultants spreading equipment, products, operating traditions, rules, methods, procedures and philosophies throughout the earth. New corporations are emerging almost everywhere. As these new corporate tribes take root and grow, they continue to draw manpower from the surrounding crop land. The population has become redistributed into dense city clusters. We are forming new tribes, new clusters of food-getters, in ways more like primitive, hunting-gathering tribes than the churches and armies of the agricultural era.

In the United States, where corporations are most numerous, the farming communities in the heartlands are deteriorating.

The streets are dusty, the buildings dilapidated, the young people escaping, the farmers aging and increasingly dependent upon the corporations that buy their crops.

Corporations did not set out to undermine or destroy the institutions and traditions of the agricultural age. But the new adaptation to territory is causing a rapid erosion of many of the concepts our grandfathers cherished.

The Machine Man

Machines, more than anything else, have changed the corporate tribesman's relationships to territory. The dramatic changes in communication and transportation make corporate man different from all his predecessors on the six million-year-old family tree. Machines influence almost every aspect of modern man's daily life.

Automobiles, television, computers, airplanes, refrigerators, telephones, snowmobiles, microscopes, outboard engines, electric ranges, tractors, electric light bulbs, trains, wristwatches, factories bursting at the seams with drills, presses, mixers, shears and hoists; elevators, typewriters, rockets, the bomb—all are very recent additions to man's environment.

One hundred years is an instant in the multi-million year time frame of man's evolution. But in one hundred years, machines have already begun to change man in fundamental ways. Machines have changed the nature of work. They have eliminated the pain of physical labor for millions of workers. Machines have helped to shift the population from agricultural farms and villages into cities, both by providing factory jobs and by eliminating farm labor.

Machines now transport man, keep him warm or cool, educate him, entertain him, provide life support when he is ill, solve problems for him, help him plant, harvest, process, cook and prepare his food.

Machines are clearly helping man to survive. We are controlling disease better and living longer, and our ability to bring offspring to maturity has never been so reliable. Machines are educating us faster and better than ever before. No longer are the secrets of science locked up in libraries and reserved for elite intellectuals who can wade through the formulas and scientific jargon. Now they are presented, predigested and summarized, to millions of TV students. The latest findings of modern science are fed into the homes of millions. Machines have given us greater mastery over our territory than men have ever known before.

But the existence of machines as a ubiquitous part of our environment has the effect of changing man. Machines are changing our work, our play, our relationships, our religions, our customs, our taboos, our education and our territorial ties. They are changing war, politics, and governments.

Machines create an accelerated scrambling of peoples and cultures. Modern transportation dramatically expands the perimeter of the machine man's territory. He no longer marries the girl next door. Thousands no longer marry or live within their family tribe, their religion, or their race.

For millions of years, tribes evolved, generation after generation, growing ever more attuned to their territories. The survival struggle screened out certain tribes, and multiplied and replenished the offspring of others.

Now suddenly, modern transportation and communications are scrambling cultures, mixing peoples together, blending and homogenizing them into fewer rather than more diverse ethnic groups.

The Automobile

Who could have predicted what the automobile has done for us and to us? How thoroughly it has changed us, and is still changing the world. A million miles of tangled, criss-crossed ribbons of asphalt and cement. Giant industries for gasoline, oil, tires, cars, iron, steel, insurance and scrap metal. Traffic jams, commuting to the suburbs, decay of the central cities, sex education in the back seat, drive-in movies, banks and hamburgers. Parking—underground, in special buildings, in huge cement lots, on streets. Parking tickets, traffic court, traffic deaths, pollution. Trucking for mass movement of goods—and the most amazing mobility ever known.

Which of our great-grandfathers, as he rolled his wagon across the bumps and sagebrush of the plains, could have dreamed that in a hundred years the shiny metal machines would be streaking smoothly at 80 miles per hour on wide flat trails, in all seasons and all weather, their passengers listening to fine orchestras or news of the world, the air and temperature metered to preserve maximum comfort. Machines within machines. No sultan, no king, no Alexander or Caesar ever experienced the speed, mobility, communications, and comfort that the average, middle-class, machine man takes so much for granted.

The automobile is directly influencing man's evolution. Anything in an environment which systematically restricts offspring from a given group will, over a period of time, influence the direction of evolution, and automobiles are doing just that.

The connecting link between one generation and the next is, literally, a river of sperm. Anything which influences the flow of sperm, turns it off or on, determines the direction evolution will take.

For example, in a tribe that exists in the same territory as man-eating tigers, those who are skilled enough to survive would contribute more children to the next generation than those who are killed before or during childbearing years.

This special environmental situation favors genetic transmission of traits related to alertness (the ability to avoid tigers). Those who survive gradually become better at dealing with tigers with each succeeding generation. Unfortunately, the tigers also evolve. Only those which survive the hunter carry on the species.

Traffic accidents are the fourth major cause of death in the United States, following heart disease, cancer, and stroke. By killing off about 613 people per week in the United States, automobiles are acting as a systematic screen to the natural processes of evolution. Many of the 613, for one reason or another, are poor drivers. They may drink too much, drive too fast, have slow reaction time, poor vision or inaccurate depth perception.

Insurance rates confirm that young drivers are more accident prone than others. Many die before they bear children. Thus, automobiles are functioning as a selection device which culls out drivers who do a poor job at operating high speed machinery.

Of course, fatally bad drivers take a random sample of other drivers, good and bad, with them. But the principle remains; poor drivers are screened out in relatively larger numbers.

As the process continues worldwide, a few hundred thousand deaths per year, over several hundred years, man will gradually become more compatible with his automobile-infested environment. This small percentage of fatalities works like compound interest tables. Each succeeding generation becomes a little more suited to living with and operating automobiles.

Television

Television may have a more profound influence on man than any other machine. Television destroys old territorial boundaries and creates new ones based on language. As McLuhan pointed out, the new television village includes everyone who has electricity, a TV set, and can understand the language being spoken.

Children in Alabama, Oregon, Hawaii, New York City and Utah receive the same stimulus input when they watch Sesame Street. Most of them absorb over 1,000 hours of TV conditioning per year. In some cases, they receive more input from the TV than they receive at school.

The varied cultural values and religious beliefs that exist in homes are brushed aside by television programming. CBS and NBC have captured the air time from Mom and Dad. All who watch receive the same message laced with the same values. We learn from what we pay attention to, and TV holds much of our attention.

John Kennedy's assassination pulled us all to the television screen, plunged us into a shared experience of murder, of mourning, of investigation and suspicion. The TV guided us to the suspected assassin, then displayed his murder for all to see. Kennedy's funeral was, by far, the largest tribal ceremony in the history of mankind.

Films from Vietnam, films of man's first landing on the moon, photographs of Mars, all have the same massive impact. In a thousand years, people may feel that the useful study of history began with the invention of the camera. What fantastic historical documents TV tapes have become. Wouldn't it be great to have videotape records of Columbus's landing?

The Olympics, with the aid of satellites, is yet another worldwide ceremony.

The TV set pumps its stimulus into thousands of cities, farms, and villages, cutting across racial, religious and geographic barriers. We all are sent the same message, are given the same lessons about the good guys and the bad guys, see the same news presentations about crises, disasters and world events.

By providing the same stimulus input to villages and towns from London to the Kentucky hills, TV is breaking down divergent traditions, belief systems and concepts of the world. The networks have added to and pre-empted the traditional transmitters of culture—families, tribal elders, teachers and religious leaders.

So, while television educates us, enculturates us, and keeps us aware of major events occurring worldwide, it also pre-empts family interaction, and by so doing, exerts a subtle yet powerful influence on the quality of our close relationships. Family relationships become shallow when TV dominates everyone's attention. Television captures our time. We sit in a semicircle now, around our new technicolor teacher, entertainer, information source. TV creates robot spectators.

Instead of talking to one another, discussing things, explaining ideas, millions now sit silently, watching. The husband spends his weekends watching football rituals. The wife spends weekdays eavesdropping on the juicy lives of TV soap opera characters. And the children absorb thousands of hours of cartoon conditioning. For many of us, our relationships with these machines are more interesting, more entertaining, more effective in capturing our attention than the people with whom we live. We are machine dependent, and as our dependency increases, the quality of interpersonal relationships probably decreases.

Television also tunes our taste for drama and musical entertainment. We all become connoisseurs. So much so, that only the best artists are acceptable to us. We no longer entertain one another at home. Thousands are embarrased to share their talents, because the audience has become accustomed to excellence. Fewer and fewer families sing together or attempt to entertain one another. We have yielded the responsibility for entertainment to a few experts.

In addition to soaking up our attention and assuming responsibility for entertainment, television also provides mock wars. Professional sports allow modern man to experience modified tribal battles without getting hurt. He can scream, cheer, and feel the emotions of conflict without risking pain or property loss. The mock battles are a shallow, essentially ceremonial, tribal warfare.

The popularity of TV football in the United States is a major phenomenon, and as yet, poorly understood. It consumes billions of man hours. Yet it is very new. The amazing growth of interest in TV sports suggests that they fulfill some deep and basic human needs. They may be harmless, vicarious outlets for man's innate tendencies for tribal warfare.

Does television violence encourage violent behavior? The reverse may be true. Modern man may be exposed to less actual violence and bloodshed than his father and grandfathers. Television may provide outlets which drain off much of modern man's primitive feelings of hostility and aggression.

The influence of TV on politics is also profound. It's likely that top politicians will increasingly be selected on the basis of the show-biz image they project on television. Screen tests, set design and makeup will become critical to the success of national leaders.

The founding fathers knew nothing about television. They had no idea that candidates for public office could be defeated because they had a poor makeup man, or because public attitudes and support could be molded by influential TV personalities. The recent ascension of a professional actor to the presidency underlines the importance of image in the age of TV.

Television is a new force in politics. Its power and influence are profound. Never in his wildest dreams would ex-president Nixon have believed that White House tapes of private conversations with his staff would serve as a script for professional actors who would recreate the scene, word for word, in front of millions of television viewers. Most politicians would shudder at the idea of conducting private business with their closest advisors in front of national TV cameras. But through the magic of electronics, Nixon's most private sessions were thus displayed.

The checks and balances built into government by the founding fathers did not anticipate anything like television. Yet, policy makers from major networks may have as much influence on the course of government events as the Congress, the Administration, or the Supreme Court. When a president says good night after delivering a major message, the next face you see is a news commentator. Often, his first words are: "There is nothing new in the President's message . . ." Before people have had time to think about their leader's message, a non-elected TV commentator tells us what he said. In this way, the leadership effect of elected officials is influenced by men who control the channels of information.

We understand little about how TV is influencing us. We go home after our day at the office, turn on the tube, and watch

Ted Koppel, Dan Rather, McNeil and Lehrer. Many of our elected leaders come and go in four or eight-year patches of time, but men like David Brinkley, Walter Cronkite and Eric Severeid seem to go on forever.

These familiar men explain and describe events of the extended tribe. They are the new TV elders of our national tribe. We go to work during the day. We spend eight hours "hunting for food" in the corporate situation, then we go home and watch TV. Television has replaced the evening entertainment — dances, meetings and ceremonies — that existed in earlier tribes.

The familiar personalities on television may also supplement our friendships. Even though we move from one city to another, we can still turn on Johnny Carson and feel a sort of continuity of friendships with Johnny, Ed and Doc.

Prior to our new industrial tribes, men all over the world supplemented their ordinary relationships with an extensive collection of spirits. These spirits had personalities. Some were kind and loving, some vengeful and easily angered. Some were evil. These spirit personalities were often present at rituals and ceremonies. Prayers and conversations with them were common.

In his article entitled "Media Mentors"[36], John L. Caughey suggests that TV characters may in fact replace this crowd of spirit personalities that previously existed in tribes.

Modern man no longer interacts with gods of the forest, rain, volcanoes or animals. But he is quite likely to supplement his day-to-day relationships with TV heroes and personalities. Many viewers carry on unacknowledged communications with TV personalities: disagreeing with newscasters, scolding talk-show hosts, and joining in with pithy comments as they munch their ham sandwiches.

As we use machines, as we communicate with them, ride in them and work with them, they change us. Do they make us blind, cold or mechanical? Why do people frequently freeze up or begin to talk in a mechanical way when dictating or talking into tape recorders?

The voice on the public address system talks like a machine. The announcements are mechanical. They never say, "Mr. Anderson, I just received a call from Mr. Jones while you were having coffee, and he wants you to call him." Instead, a monotone machine voice, accompanied by buzzes or ding-dings, announces: "Mr. Anderson, plee-uzz call extension three-oh-ni-unn."

The man on the assembly line moves like the machine he tends: A prescribed series of automatic jerks and pulls. The secretary bangs away at her typewriter all day, while her boss dictates more typing into still another machine.

The shallow relationships and diminishing emotional spontaneity of modern men and women may be a by-product of their growing intimacy with machines. The automobile is a metal compartment which links his home compartment with his work compartment. Commuting in machines helps keep his life compartmentalized. He makes the drive twice a day, sealed in a machine. He usually drives alone.

Mass transit studies confirm our growing dependence on automobiles. We're reluctant to switch to cheaper, more efficient ways of transit because our to-and-from time is a time we get to be "alone", and we are reluctant to give it up.

One of the accidental results of modern corporate life is that most of us work with one collection of personalities and play with another. Neither set gets to know us very well. The weekend crowd thinks you're a bit flaky—you're often at a party when you're with them. And the weekday office personalities see you as sober and hard working.

Corporations, automobiles, suburbs, and freeways seal modern man into compartmentalized life styles. In the city, he associates with people who put on the corporate tribal costume every day. When they see him he is always wearing a suit and tie, playing his businessman role, talking about sales, profits, projects, reports and business problems.

At the end of his eight-hour performance he returns home, changes costumes, and plays the father, neighbor or husband role. The sets change. The other actors change. Modern man lives with a series of separate and less-continuous relationships than his predecessors. By definition, his relationships are more shallow.

Corporate Nomads

Corporate man has transient attachments to specific patches of land, compared with his recent ancestors. Most of the billions of men who have populated the earth have lived and died, played out every chapter of their lives, within the territory of a few square miles. As with the American Indians, separation from tribal territory often led to disease and death.

Modern men and women are far more adaptable. They live a few years in one place, then they truck their belongings to someplace new.

★ ★ ★

As a small child, Fred Reed lived on Maple Avenue in St. Louis. Linden Avenue, the next street over, was a strange, faraway place. The young boys his age who lived on Linden seemed dangerous to him—a bit threatening—the enemy.

As Fred grew older, Linden and the kids who lived there became safe and familiar. But he was suspicious of the boys on Michigan Avenue who attended a different grade school.

Junior high school, once again, pushed out the boundaries of his environment. The circumference of Fred's life space expanded. So did his circle of friends. At East High School, it happened again. Now the enemies were those rough greasers from West High.

First the bicycle, then the automobile had a profound impact on the circumference of Fred's territory. At age 5, a trip in the car downtown with his parents seemed like an endless drive. At age 16, he cruised that distance several times a day, slouched in the front seat of his buddy's car, sneering at the West High stranger-enemies, trying to be cool when they passed girls on the street.

The perimeter of the territory Fred regularly covered in 1958 America probably exceeded the world norm for adult men, living and dead. Taking into account the millions who played out their entire lives within the narrow limits of a tribal hunting territory, the average teenager of today is widely traveled.

By age thirty-five, Fred had lived in St. Louis, New York, Chicago, Cleveland, Houston, and Minneapolis. Such mobility is common among corporate tribesmen.

★　　　★　　　★

This mobility, looked at in the context of the territorial ties of all the previous ages of mankind, is new. In a sense, the corporate tribesman has returned to a new sort of nomadic lifestyle, detached from an intimate life-and-death relationship to a specific patch of food-providing territory.

Tribal territory is now a matter of office space, carefully measured and awarded to tribesmen of the new hive-like high-rise tribal villages. The new territorial rules tend to concentrate us in cities during the day. Rather than periodically return from the fields or the hunt to the cluster of familiar tribal personalities in the evening or on weekends, the corporate tribesmen disperse to the anonymity of homes in suburbs and residential neighborhoods. Those who live nearby are often total strangers. His home, like his office, reflects his success in the struggle for territory. But his most continuous and closest relationships, shallow though they may be, are often those he forms at work.

In almost any corporate meeting, the reality of modern man's re-emerging nomadism can be easily demonstrated. Ask the assembled group of executives to list all the cities where they have lived, where they were born, where they grew up. One invariably comes away with the sensation of having been tossed into a randomly shuffled collection of people. They come from everywhere. Most have spent chapters of their lives in a variety of cities and towns. At top executive levels this nomadism is especially prevalent.

Many corporate pyramids are made up of near strangers, employees who rarely see one another outside the office. When two executives meet at work, they cover points one, two, and three of their mutual business, and it's back to work. They are sitting in business offices. The setting is the same. This little window of a relationship tells executives very little about one another.

The more frequently a machine man is transferred by his corporation, the more frequently he moves to accept a new job opportunity, the more his ties to traditional tribal life are influenced. Ties to the church, the tribal congregation, the group singing, his parents, relatives and friends are left behind. The more frequently the modern executive moves, the more the corporation emerges as his tribe. It becomes the group to which he gives top priority commitment.

The corporate tribe often dominates other tribal ties. Other ties are partially sacrificed when one moves. Executives often leave it all behind. Their career takes priority. The corporate tribe emerges as the focus for one's primary loyalties.

Shrinking Family Clusters

A family in the hunting-gathering tribe was a large group of people, often matriarchal, made up of many children, aunts, uncles and grandparents, all living in the same village.

Farming resulted in a more thin distribution of people across the crop land. Agriculture and the emergence of the "father" role resulted in smaller family units. Families in agricultural times were a man, his wife and their children. But they generally lived close enough to uncles and aunts and grandparents to assemble for ceremonies, celebrations, the harvest and church meetings. The residents of small-town farming villages kept close track of one another. They traced the births, deaths, marriages and life histories of other townspeople. But the actual family cluster of agricultural man was much smaller than the clan group of the hunter-gatherer.

Corporate tribesmen move a great deal, and this return to a more nomadic lifestyle has resulted in another fracturing of the family cluster. Now we have an even smaller family group. It normally includes a man, his wife and their children, but the grandparents are no longer present. The uncles and aunts are often hundreds of miles away. For divorced managers, now a large percentage of executives, family structures include only one parent.

Psychologists are realizing that the relationship a child has with its grandparents is special. In terms of the "I'm O.K., You're O.K." philosophies, it is a particularly nourishing relationship—particularly healthy for growing children. Grandparents can often see nothing wrong with their grandchildren. They shower affection on them. In the mind of the grandparent, the child is O.K. "You're O.K." they say, over and over, in their smiles and hugs. These healthy and soothing pats on the back enhance confidence and self-esteem.

Recent figures indicate that 54% of the working-age women in the U.S. are now in the labor force. Once again, the children of modern men are being separated from a relationship that was closer and more continuous for pre-technological children.

No one knows what is happening to modern children who grow up without the extended family relationships. It's another new phenomenon. Perhaps we will no longer need these relationships. We may become more cool, independent, and indifferent toward one another. We know that thousands of relationships with parents, grandparents, aunts, uncles, and cousins have been curtailed. The increasing number of divorces and single-parent families provides more dramatic evidence of the trend away from traditional family life.

Children in hunting and agricultural tribes had many personalities with whom to relate, many adult role models from which to learn. They could observe adults at work, and imitate adult occupations. They were eager to join the hunt, milk the cow, and drive the team. These experiences provided a learning climate which offered many models of adult behavior.

The widespread negative opinions about entering corporate life that are encountered on college campuses may be a by-product of separating young people from adult role models involved in corporate activities.

Children of corporate workers see their parents leave in the morning and return in the evening. Modern children have comparatively few opportunities to observe groups of adults working together in corporate settings, except perhaps on television.

The conditioning for shallow interpersonal relationships starts early for modern children. When their only continuous relationship during early years is with their mother, both the mother and the child may suffer a sort of overload. Margaret Mead indicated that in Samoa, both mothers and children benefited from help in child-rearing provided by grandparents and young unmarried girls.[37]

High divorce rates in industrialized countries may also be related to the disintegration of family size. Without the extended families of tribal life and the farming villages, married couples may overload their relationships and look to each other to satisfy all their interpersonal needs. They may place unrealistic demands on one another and seek, in their only remaining close relationship, all the variety, entertainment, and involvement that used to be provided by many people of the tribe.

Children of many corporate executives, like their parents, are uprooted from family ties, church ties, community ties and friendships when dad changes companies or is transferred. They see more of the country when they move from place to place, and they can usually establish contact with new churches, clubs, and community groups, but their relationships do not build and grow with the same consistency and endurance as those of precorporate children. What they gain in variety of friends, they may sacrifice in long and enduring relationships.

Modern children become involuntary nomads when their parents accept a transfer which requires relocation. They lose the benefits of grandparent affection, association with cousins, uncles and aunts, and long term friendships. They may begin a conditioning process that makes them more able to adapt to a nomadic lifestyle when they complete their adolescence, go through their rites-of-passage, and themselves become corporate tribes-people.

Territorial Control as a Zero-Sum Game

For early man, the same patch of territory might provide food for several hunting-gathering tribes, depending on the population of game and tribesmen. When hunting parties encountered one another, skirmishes often resulted. But when territory provided crops, loss of control often meant slavery, starvation or death. There was nothing complicated about it. In agricultural times, loss of a territorial war often meant slaughter of the adult males, and slavery for the women and children. Slaves were people separated from their territory by conquest.

In psychology, games like Monopoly, checkers and poker are zero-sum games. In a zero-sum game, someone has to lose. As world population increased, the control of food-producing territory began to evolve into a zero-sum game. Territory, especially fertile cropland, is limited. What one tribe wins, another must lose.

Agricultural man was involved in especially competitive life and death zero-sum games. Conflict was probably inevitable. Organized warfare—first with hordes, then trained armies—is an agricultural institution, the result of competition for valuable but limited food-producing cropland.

As corporate tribes emerged, the multiple use of territory became possible. The same patch of territory could now be exploited by many corporate tribes without armed conflict. Tribal villages could actually be stacked on top of one another in the new highrise office complexes.

The motivation to invade Mexico and Canada, to battle for crop territory, clearly eased as the U.S. population became converted into corporate tribespeople.

Armies first emerged during the rise of agriculture, as did complex governments and the first civilizations. The emergence of new tribal forms that can exchange a variety of goods and services for food have created new non-military forms of competition for survival. Power has shifted from the control of food-producing territory to the control of capital, raw materials, markets, channels of communication, labor and technology. Hot wars with armies of retrained farmers are no longer inevitable. They may fade, just as cannibalism, headhunting and slavery have faded.

When U.S. consumers first fell in love with Volkswagens, the German economy took a dramatic surge. The same thing happened in Japan when the American sales volume of Hondas and Toyotas began to swell.

Similarly, during the recessions of the early 1970s and 1980s when the U.S. economy had bad years, shock waves echoed all over the world.

Thus, nation-states which were once bitter rivals now want U.S. corporate tribes to be healthy. They need U.S. consumers to continue buying their products.

If Arabs, Canadians or Japanese had attempted to occupy prime areas of U.S. or European cropland in our grandfather's generation, they would have been vigorously opposed by armed and uniformed soldiers. The man on the street in Minneapolis seemed surprised to discover that Canadians had purchased several large chunks of prime downtown real estate. He did not realize that thousands of acres of prime U.S. property are now owned by foreign individuals and corporations. U.S. corporations have owned and controlled thousands of acres of territory in other nation–states since the early stages of the Industrial Revolution.

The old meaning of nation-state, a patch of food-producing territory, defended by an army of national warriors, may fade as nation after nation industrializes.

In the modern world, the territory and resources of an industrialized nation-state are actually owned by corporations and individuals from many nation-states. As long as these foreign owners obey the law and pay their taxes, all is well.

It is clear that industrialization has caused some dramatic changes in the territorial zero-sum game. Foreign ownership of local territory is no longer feared. For the informed corporate tribesman, it is actually encouraged. It is recognized as a powerful form of insurance against armed conflict. Most major corporations own and control territory in many nation-states. They recognize that armed conflict hurts business, restricts investment and curtails corporate growth.

These massive economic forces may signal an end to the zero-sum games of the agricultural era. An awareness of a growing and deeply entrenched economic interdependency within the world may allow our ancient, single-minded appetite for cropland and hunting territory to fade.

The Berlin Wall, like the Great Wall of China, is an expression of an agricultural mentality. Large standing armies and war are institutions of the agricultural age. As that age passes, armies will become ceremonial, vestigial organs of governments. They will slowly fade away as science, corporations, and international trade grows.

It will not be a sudden process. Although hunting and gathering tribes have been fading away since agriculture emerged 10,000 years ago—and more rapidly with recent exposure to machines—many continue to survive.

War will not disappear out of humanistic motives. It will no longer contribute to the survival and growth of the new tribes. Skill at controlling resources, including raw materials, sources of capital, human resources, machines and knowledge, will gradually replace military conquest as corporations grow and agricultural societies continue to evolve into industrialized societies. The boundaries of the nation-states, defined with much bloodshed by our agricultural forefathers, no longer exclude tribesmen of foreign corporations. Neither do they contain the tribesmen of U.S. corporations.

Survival and growth of corporate tribes is measured by growth in employment, as well as by profits. It depends on sales, production costs and efficient administration. It does not depend on fire power, bombs, armies or skill at hunting and war.

But, until world markets are more firmly established, until the masses of farm workers in the developing nations of the world are successfully converted into well-educated and well-paid industrial tribesmen, until the number of troops, generals and war machines decreases, the danger of more wars will continue. The danger will be greatest among nations which are least industrialized.

Throughout history, technological advances have helped one tribe or federation of tribes conquer, destroy, subjugate or enslave another. The Hittite discovery of iron shifted the balance of power. Those without iron were overrun and destroyed. Metal armor and horses helped the Conquistadores subjugate Central America. With 200 men armed with rifles, Stanley trespassed over one African tribal territory after another, inflicting death on any warriors who dared to oppose him.

Predatory men with a technological advantage have been subjugating others and using their resources for a long time. Stanley recounts his meeting with Tippu-Tib, a sultan of Zanzibar.[38]

> *"Tippu-Tib . . . actually had three Krupp shells, unloaded, which he had brought with him from Stanley Falls, on the Upper Congo, to Zanzibar, to exhibit to his friends as the kind of missile which the Belgians pelted his settlements with—and he was exceedingly wroth, and nourished a deep scheme of retaliation."*

The carpet bombing of Vietnam villages, with weapons more powerful than Stanley could have imagined, is a more recent example of the predatory behavior of armies.

Modern nations still need a strong and technologically superior military to secure territorial integrity. But the arena for world competition has shifted from raw troop count, required to capture cropland and secure territory, to competition for business, raw materials, labor, markets, television air time, and capital.

Today's aggressive method for reducing bloodshed and eliminating war in the world is to actively nourish developing corporations throughout the world—creating products, jobs, trained labor, markets, communications, transportation—in short, industrialization and technology. The computers Control Data recently sold to Red China were tokes from a very powerful peacepipe. Reagan's attempt to limit the development of the Russian pipe line slowed the steady progress toward world peace.

Marshall McLuhan[39] recognized the passing of the war age;

> *"Whenever hot wars are necessary these days, we conduct them in the back yards of the world with the old technologies. These wars are happenings, tragic games. It is no longer convenient, or suitable, to use the latest technologies for fighting our wars, because the latest technologies have rendered war meaningless. The hydrogen bomb is history's exclamation point. It ends an age-long sentence of manifest violence."*

The atomic bomb was the turning point. Korea and Vietnam were tragic pseudo-wars, waged against rice farmers on someone else's cropland by men who had no intention of actually occupying the conquered territory. They were philosophical, ideological wars.

Now that corporate life is replacing farming as the daily activity for large masses of population, bloodshed is no longer necessary for growth and survival. In fact, it disrupts corporate markets and inhibits growth.

Territory for Corporate Tribes

In Europe, Asia, North and South America, India, Australia and Japan—wherever farming men and women built permanent homes in the fields, away from cities, tribal activities became more occasional. Families could survive independently, by growing their own food and raising their own animals. Their tribal affiliations were primarily religious or political in nature, and more intensive tribal activity surfaced only during worship or war.

But modern corporate employees spend five days a week, eight hours a day, in large, food-getting clusters. They form departments, groups of working teams. In this respect, corporate employees are more like hunter-gatherers than their farming-oriented fathers or grandfathers.

In the past one hundred years, we have been reorganizing into new kinds of tribes. This requires less individual and more team-oriented survival activity. In essence, we may be unconsciously reestablishing some elements of tribal life that were suppressed during the 10,000-year era of agriculture.

Corporate organizations are our new tribal affiliations. We still affiliate with churches and nation states as did our farmer grandparents. But corporate affiliations are something new, powerful and compelling. They replace the thousands of hours men and women of our recent past spent alone in the fields, or perhaps with one or two close relatives, tending their crops and animals.

Corporations, by pulling together new clusters of working teams, are like hunting-gathering tribes, in that success depends more on team effort and less on individual effort.

Modern man is still a highly territorial beast. Like his predecessors, he is attentive to several key patches of territory. The first is his home. Its size and location reflect his position in the corporate pecking order. Within his home are common territories (the kitchen, living room and family room), and private territories (the bedrooms). As its name implies, the master bedroom is the private domain of the master and his wife. Many men are quite willing to kill intruders who might unexpectedly break into this private domain.

In addition to his home territory, corporate man also has an office. This is his assigned tribal territory. It reflects his position in the tribal pecking order. For this reason the reshuffling of office space within corporations usually reflects changes in the corporate pecking order. When some executive gains or slips a notch in the corporate pecking order, the reassignment of his office is proof positive of new status within the tribe.

In addition to his home and his office territories, modern man is also attentive to the political boundaries of his nation–state. When these are threatened, he behaves like his agricultural forefathers who conquered earlier inhabitants and secured the land. He joins or is drafted into the army to defend the territory. Not only do modern nation–states maintain an active force of trained warriors and soldiers, they remain ready to convert corporate employees to warriors when serious challenges to their territorial sovereignty occur.

But serious challenges and disputes about territory of nation–states seem to exist primarily within and between underdeveloped countries, those which have large populations of citizens involved in farming. Industrialized nation–states compete in new and different ways.

The weapons of war have changed dramatically since the day our agricultural forefathers abandoned their plows to take up arms. Wars are now fought continually, but without bloodshed or armies. They are waged with sales representatives, market shares, lines of credit, low interest loans and the manipulation of prices and supplies.

Corporations divide territory into sales regions. These evolved hunting grounds are similar to the food-providing areas of hunting-gathering tribes. But the diversity of products and services which are sold within any given geographical area allows the same patch of territory to be worked by hundreds of different corporate hunters without direct conflict. A salesman can get into serious trouble with his tribe by prospecting outside of his assigned territory, and the competition for shares of the market between organizations with similar products can be very aggressive. But corporations do not claim sovereignty or control over sales regions, and competition between salesmen of different corporations excludes bloodshed.

★   ★   ★

Karen Smith (a fictitious name but a true story) was a relatively new sales representative for General Mills. She called on grocery stores. Her territory was northwest Wisconsin. (Because she is the oldest daughter of close friends, and because I am intensely curious about the many women who are becoming corporate sales representatives, I have followed her career.)

Shelf space is the main arena for battle among the various corporate representatives who sell to grocery stores. One day, during a sales call, Karen aggressively expanded her shelf space for Wheaties in a small Mom and Pop grocery store. The eye level shelf is the best, and Karen replaced some of the Post Cornflakes with her own product.

Unfortunately, the Post representative, a six-foot-four ex-football player, arrived at the store before Karen left. When he saw what she had done he was more than a bit annoyed. "Who changed my shelf space?" he bellowed, loud enough so that Mom, Pop, and several customers clearly heard his complaint. So did Karen. "I did," she retorted. "You wanna step outside and talk about it?"

The twinkle of humor in her eye was probably unexpected. It broke the ice. She and the ex-football player, combatants for their separate corporate tribes, became friends. Karen kept the prime eye-level shelf space. She was an effective corporate hunter, a valuable warrior in the battle for market share.

★   ★   ★

The new, more subtle warfare of the corporate tribe involves salesmanship and persuasion. Although it excludes open conflicts, fights or bloodshed, it is helpful to develop and maintain enough ruthlessness to compete successfully.

Other patches of territory owned or controlled by corporations usually include raw material sources, such as mineral deposits, timberland, and oil fields, in addition to the land on which the plants and headquarters offices are located. These patches of territory are frequently fenced, secured and defended as vigorously as was the crop land or village compound of more primitive tribes. Corporate employees carry no weapons. They are almost never asked to take up arms to defend corporate property. When corporate facilities have been nationalized, great fortunes have been lost, but relatively little blood was shed. In earlier times, troops were sometimes dispatched to protect the assets of a nation's corporations, but economic sanctions are now more likely to be imposed, and are often more effective.

Summary

Corporations have a new relationship to territory that may be as deep and profound as was the change from hunting and gathering to agriculture. After only 100 years, we are probably seeing only the beginning of these changes. But already there are indications of parallels with the earlier change. Among other things, the change from hunting and gathering to agriculture changed the nature of war, the nature of family structures, the patterns of population density and man's concepts of God and religion. These appear to be happening again. More research is needed to clarify what happens to people when a major change in their basic relationship to territory occurs.

Corporate man, by working in larger teams than his agri-culturally oriented predecessors, and by forming into clusters during the day rather than dispersing into the fields, may be adopting tribal characteristics that have been dormant or in remission during the 10,000 year era of agriculture.

Underlying these changes there are also continuities, things that seemed to remain unchanged through the earlier adaptation from hunting-gathering to agriculture. One of these is man's basic tribal nature. Chapter III, On the Evolution of Tribal Roles, suggests that these continuities may be far more com-pelling, detailed, and enduring elements of man's basic nature than we have previously realized.

Chapter Three

ON THE EVOLUTION OF TRIBAL ROLES

DARWIN supported his controversial theories by suggesting that an analysis of the developing fetus may well give hints to stages of an organism's evolutionary history. In its first weeks the developing human fetus looks reptilian, then bird-like, with an enlarged head and prominent eye spots. Later it looks like other mammals, complete with a tail. As it develops, it becomes more complex and more differentiated. The process may recapitulate millions of years of evolutionary development. To describe the process, Darwin used the phrase "ontogeny recapitulates phylogeny".

The principle may also apply to evolving human groups. As human clusters evolved down through the ages, they obviously became more complex and differentiated. But each new complexity may have evolved from earlier, simpler, less differentiated forms. Modern corporations require an amazing array of specialized jobs. Earlier tribes had fewer jobs or tasks. They were less complex. It is possible that all modern roles, all jobs in the corporate tribe, can be traced back through the twigs and branches of the agriculture era, to earlier hunter-gatherer adaptations.

Anthropologists have recognized similarities between corporations and tribes for years. But few members of the Board of Directors realize, as they assemble in their Board Room, that they are the modern expression of the council of elders, an organization form that has been identified in primitive tribes in Africa, Australia, South America, Polynesia, New Guinea, the Philippines, among American Indians — all over the world. And few businessmen who gather for lunch at the Athletic Club realize that their meeting facility, including its taboos against women, is much like the men's huts of primitive tribes observed by Margaret Mead in Samoa, by Malinowski in the South Pacific, Claude Levi–Strauss in the Amazon basin, Colin Turnbull in Africa, and Kilton Stewart in Luzon.

The terms "financial wizard," "high-powered attorney" and "head shrinker" may be more than jokes. They may reveal a half-buried awareness that outside experts who are called into corporations are a modern expression of the archetypal tribal role of shaman.

One of the difficulties in tracing the evolution of tribal roles is that the 10,000-year era of agriculture stands between us and earlier tribal forms. This era of the farmer may present a dark glass which clouds the vision of our hunter-gatherer roots.

I have come to believe that all of us who are employed by large modern corporations are, in fact, performing tasks and duties for our companies that have ancient origins.

This chapter will trace several of the most basic tribal roles. We will see how they evolved during the agriculture era and in what form they surfaced again in corporate tribes.

The Hunter

Most adult males in the multi-million year history of Homo sapiens were hunters. Tribes survived and grew, or deteriorated and failed, according to their hunters' skill at obtaining meat. The act of killing yielded immense reward for the hunter, not only in providing food but also in the adulation and praise of his tribe. In many hunting-gathering cultures the hunter was expected to re-tell his adventure in the form of ceremonial dances so his tribe could share in his success, and admire his prowess.

For hunter-gatherers, meat was money. The great hunter, by sharing his meat with others, created repayable obligations. Tribesmen admired and emulated those who consistently succeeded in obtaining meat.

For men in early hunter-gatherer tribes, career planning was a snap. Men became hunters, women became gatherers. Almost everyone was expected to fulfill one of these primary roles. For the male child, preparation for the hunt began early. Play activities provided training for the hunt. As the male child grew, the systematic reward of hunting skills—courage, speed, endurance, an understanding of the habits of the food animals, skill in the use of weapons, skill in tracking—all prepared him for his adult career. The privilege of joining adult males in the hunt represented a major benchmark in a young man's career. This recognition was celebrated in rites-of-passage ceremonies. Sometimes receiving his first weapons was also an occasion for celebration, another significant benchmark. Success in rearing hunters was critical. The survival of the tribe depended on it.

Most hunters were occasional or part-time warriors. Sporadic skirmishes to capture or defend hunting territory were the rule rather than the exception among early hunting-gathering peoples.

A small percentage of males who were physically or temperamentally unsuited to hunting and warfare were sometimes ridiculed and assigned tribal duties that were typically female.

As tribes evolved, the number and variety of roles increased. As agriculture took root, a new set of survival skills was overlaid on the hunters' roles. But most farmers still retained their interest in hunting and war. In many tribes, much of the planting and tending of crops and domestic animals became a female duty. The adult males continued to travel away from the bivouac, sometimes covering large territories, to provide meat.

As we have seen, the role of soldier, the full-time warrior, emerged with agriculture. In farming cultures, including those of Europe, China, Japan and India, the full-time soldier evolved into a special class, a cut above that of the farmer. The fact that most farmers continued to hunt, and would periodically leave the fields to join the army and defend or expand their political tribe's territorial control, shows that the mainstream hunter-warrior role, refined over millions of years of survival, remained just beneath the surface.

Today, it is a bit further beneath the surface. The popularity of TV violence and the persistent themes of violence in children's play may reflect our innate interest in hunting and war. Our TV heroes are still violent men, skillful at killing enemies.

But industrial man's continued fervent interest in hunting, weapons and bloody war may be slightly less compelling than that of his farmer forefathers. Our modern entertainments have evolved into bloodless forms of hunting and tribal warfare. Catcher's masks and hockey sticks have replaced armor and spears. The sports activities of boys and young men still stress the importance of team skills and physical fitness. The current rage of jogging and running may be a throwback to primitive times. Anthropologists in Africa and South America have described their burning lungs and the pain they endured in trying to keep pace with primitive hunters who often ran steadily for many hours to make a kill.

In the corporate tribe, hunters have evolved into salesmen. The term, "bring home the bacon", reflects a dim recognition that the salesman, like the hunter before him, feeds the tribe.

The task of "feeding the tribe" has always been urgent. Locating herds and understanding the habits of the game have evolved into market research. Preparing traps and bait has evolved into advertising, packaging, and product design.

Extensive travel, now as always, is characteristic of the hunter. He still must cover a specific patch of food-provider territory. Now as always, his knowledge of that territory is essential to success. Modern transportation has dramatically expanded food-provider territory for the evolved hunter. Most executives are still hunters. Most of us hunt for money in the form of contracts for services, orders, budget dollars, raises, bonuses or sales. Millions of years of predator blood runs in our veins. Many of us, in a subconscious sense, are ready, if not eager, to replay the hunter-warrior role.

Delivering the death blow has evolved into closing the sale. It may still require a dose of ruthlessness, and an awareness that the needs of the tribe back home must outweigh the objections, hesitations and evasions of the customer. The flush of joy and satisfaction one feels when landing a new contract are ancient emotions.

Thousands of young men and women who enter corporations each year are, now as always, joining the hunt. They begin the process of learning about the tribe's hunting methods, the products or services, the customer, the territory and the competition. But a radical change has occurred. No blood is shed. Persuasion has replaced physical strength and endurance as an essential requirement. Tasks have become verbal rather than physical. The modern hunter carries a briefcase rather than bows, arrows, swords or rifles. Inside his briefcase are written proposals, correspondence, quantitative data, studies and reports. Reading, writing, arithmetic, and salesmanship are the basic skill requirements that must now be mastered by the developing corporate hunters.

Modern sales requires ongoing relationships, rather than accurate prey-killing shots of the bow and arrow. Top corporate salesman must establish and maintain satisfying long-term relations with their customers. The interaction is bloodless. Rather than inflict death, they try to please with fair prices, quality products, dependable delivery promises and extra services. In this sense, the activities of the corporate hunter may be seen as a combination of both hunting and farming skills. Customer relationships must be tended and nurtured as carefully as crops if they are to produce food on a regular basis.

The salesman still feeds the tribe, provides work for it, and brings in revenue that is divided among its members, exchangeable for food at the local supermarket.

In most corporations there are also super, big-game hunters. They handle big accounts, buy and sell sub-tribes, obtain financing and close major contracts. Their game is specialized. Many screen and train the newer, younger hunters. They are called sales managers, product managers, and sales vice-presidents.

In New Guinea, early observers of head-hunting rituals were shocked to observe that the victims of raids, soon to be killed and eaten, would take active roles in their own death ceremonies. They painted themselves and attached feathers, danced and played their assigned roles as they dutifully allowed themselves to be killed.

The purchasing agents of modern corporations also go along with the ritual verbal dance and allow themselves to be sold.

In corporations, those salesmen who demonstrate success in bringing home the bacon get promoted, expand their territories and take on the responsibility for recruiting and training other salesmen. Continued success leads to a larger territory. Troop count expands with continued success. In time, the sales executive "leaves the trenches". He still travels extensively, plans major campaigns and reviews progress, but the day-to-day hunting activity is left to younger men.

Slavemasters

The role of the manufacturing executive also evolved from the hunter, but in a slightly different way. In hunting-gathering times, the process of taking over a competing tribe's food-provider territory usually involved a battle of warriors. Afterward, the losing warriors were often enslaved or put to the sword. Females and children were absorbed into the winning tribe. Hunter-gatherers regarded these new tribespeople as slaves. They occupied the lowest rung of the tribe's dominance hierarchy. But they could be absorbed into the mainstream as they mastered the language and customs of their new tribe.

In agricultural times, the massive numbers of new tribes-people that resulted when one horde conquered another brought new meaning to slavery. Conquered adult males, properly controlled, also represented an important source of labor. But some of the soldiers had to be assigned to keep track of the slaves; guard them, force them to work, and direct their work projects. The skills required to perform this work were similar to the skills required to train, lead and supervise squads of soldiers. Those who supervised and led troops during war were similar to those who supervised and led slaves, but there were some key differences. The production man and the slaves he led traveled less. They performed the hardest and dirtiest work. Slaves were supervised more closely. They were paid less, usually only food and shelter, and disciplined more harshly. An adversarial relationship was a normal part of daily life, as was the necessity to make progress on large-scale farming or construction projects.

So while one group of hunters specialized in war to expand or defend food-providing territory, another specialized in supervising slave labor. After a few generations had passed, the conquered slaves became serfs, peasants and tenant farmers. In Europe landowners regularly enlisted serfs and peasants to become foot soldiers when wars erupted. This class distinction still exists in the officer versus enlisted-man of modern armies, and in the blue-collar versus salaried workers of modern corporations.

Gatherers

The daily lives and activities of gatherers are eloquently described in the book *Nisa. The Life and Words of a !Kung Woman,* by Marjorie Shostak. By learning the !Kung language and translating Nisa's tape-recorded life story, the author effectively communicates what life is like for a person who gathers for a living.

Shostak shows that among the !Kung, life is pretty good. Men and women have a good deal of leisure time. Women spend little more than two days a week in gathering. Their diets are balanced and nourishing. They have much status and autonomy. They are regarded as owners, together with men, of territorial water holes and food resources. Shostak suggests that one reason for their high status may be the major role they play in feeding their tribes. Shostak asserts that their gathering activities "account for 60 to 80 percent, by weight, of the total food consumed."[40]

The gatherers in corporations are relatively easy to identify. They are still largely women, and they fill entry level clerical roles. They still remain close to the base camp during the day and take an active role in carrying out the day-to-day functions of the tribal compound. In the corporate tribe, these gatherers do filing, typing, and yes—making and serving coffee. They are secretaries, file clerks and receptionists. These roles may have evolved from earlier roles as searchers for roots, berries and honey, as preparers of food and makers of clothing.

Searching for berries, vegetables and edible roots required a keen observation of nearby areas, and a thorough and specialized knowledge of territory different from that of a hunter. While men searched the horizon and made long journeys, women searched the land, trees and streams of nearby areas. "Accounts receivable" seems to be essentially an evolved gathering task. Telephone sales in such settings as airline reservations are powerful gathering functions.

★   ★   ★

Years ago, I had occasion to do some testing and research within a large airline reservation department. The reservations function was highly computerized. Each reservations agent was measured by the computer in a number of ways. The computer kept track of the number and length of calls handled, total ticket revenues produced, length of time off the line and between calls.

It also measured the number of people waiting on the line to talk to an agent, and the number who got tired of waiting and hung up.

During the two hours it took to pull some of the top reservations agents off the phones to take the test battery, the company estimates it lost over $100,000 in ticket sales. Reservations agents are very powerful gatherers indeed.

*   *   *

Retail shops, where sales clerks lie in wait for their prey, are a form of gathering. Advertising and displays are like brightly colored lures, designed to attract the game. Thus, much retail marketing and sales activities are like the setting of traps and snares.

The personnel department performs a gathering function, obtaining human resources. Accounts payable and payroll may be seen as protectors and preservers of tribal resources, as dividers of the meat from the hunt. Training is part of a tribe's nurturing and skills-development effort.

Our new knowledge of male bonding leads immediately to questions regarding female bonding. Are there hereditary forces at work which lead women into their own clusters, complete with pyramids and dominance hierarchies? So far, the evidence is inconclusive. In most hunting-gathering tribes, women are involved in some exclusively female ceremonies and activities. These seem to offer a counterpoint to male activities. Women's societies, professional groups, church auxiliaries, sororities, volunteer organizations and social clubs may be examples of female bonding. It appears that secretaries of top level executives occupy positions of dominance and get more pay than secretaries of lower level executives. They seem to "hitchhike" on the status of their bosses. Research is needed to explore these key questions.

It is clear that hunting and tribal wars provided a major reason for early divisions of work into sex groups. Pregnant women and those with infants were a liability on a hunt or a war party. And women in many primitive tribes were pregnant much of the time during their prime childbearing years. However, in regions where game animals were scarce, the gathering activities of tribeswomen often accounted for a majority of the food supply.

There are many examples of powerful women, priestesses, sorceresses, and female healers. The frequent occurrence of princesses, queens and heads of state demonstrates that alpha need not be male. But most of them reached power through husbands or fathers.

In some tribes men cook only for themselves, while women cook their own and their children's meals on a separate fire. Home construction is not clearly delineated. Sometimes this is done by women, sometimes by men. Central African tribal women control the lucrative grain market, and females in Japan's agricultural age handled the family finances.

Among the nomadic Indians of the American plains it was believed that women were far more suited to carrying heavy loads than men. When an encampment was moved, women did the work.

Some anthropologists have gone so far as to say that differences in biology and types of intelligence may be linked to early divisions of labor. Men, for example, are thought to have better-developed spatial intelligence than women, so fewer of them become disoriented when getting off elevators. Men walk differently, throw differently and adapt more easily to changes in temperature. These differences may be linked genetically to several million years of outdoor hunting activity.

Man's greater predatory drive is clear from prison statistics throughout much of the world. Prisons collect predators, and prison populations in the United States, as well as in most foreign countries, are 95% or higher, male. Controlled studies of differences in male and female behavior confirm that from an early age, males are more aggressive.

In many tribes, scattered in various places throughout the world, the woman's role is harsh. She often does most of the heavy work while the old man swaps hunting tales with his pals. She often undergoes elaborate ceremonies following menstruation. She is not allowed to eat many foods. Men frequently save the most desired delicacies for themselves and make them taboo for women.

In a great many tribes, women are not allowed to enter certain huts. Among the Todas of Tibet, women are not allowed to pass a small tower in front of the hut where butter is stored. Women are frequently excluded from council huts, ceremonial huts, or holy places where costumes, masks, pipes and religious props are kept.

Exclusion of females from church leadership and the military reveals how separate sex roles continued to evolve during the age of agriculture.

The men's club for corporate executives functions much like the men's hut in primitive tribes. Many have separate side entrances for women. In some, women are allowed to enter only at certain times, on certain floors, but executive men's clubs often exclude women from a majority of their facilities.

★　　　★　　　★

In Chicago in 1972, I had occasion to do some consulting work for a very competent female executive. She was the executive director of a public service organization. The partner in charge of her account and I had met with her for a progress report over lunch. We had just finished our luncheon discussion at a large, well-known, downtown men's club, and were on our way out the door when the doorman stopped us.

"The door for the ladies is down the hallway," he said.

Our client was embarrassed. So were we. We were standing six feet from the revolving door of the main entrance.

"Ladies are not supposed to be in this area," he repeated.

It was embarrassing to everyone, but not in the least

unusual. Has industrial man come a long way in elevating the status of women? In some ways his behavior toward them remains primitive.

★   ★   ★

Men are larger. They are stronger. They outperform women in most athletic events where strength, size, or speed is an advantage. As long as women have wombs and breasts, it is impossible to deny their better suitability for childbearing and rearing.

As long as men are stronger, it is difficult to deny their better suitability for tasks which require physical strength. But for the corporate executive, such tasks are rapidly diminishing. Machines are doing most of the work which requires strength, and women operate machines as well as men.

If field sales is the evolved role of the hunter, further research may demonstrate why early corporate field sales was almost exclusively a male occupation. However, when the act of obtaining food for the tribe no longer required physical strength or the shedding of blood, and instead required effective verbal persuasion, the way was opened for increasing numbers of women to pursue careers in sales. When differences in physical strength were no longer important to perform warring and hunting tasks, a major reason for separate sex roles may have disappeared. In a great many modern corporations where women have been recruited and trained in sales skills, they perform as well as men. The closing of a sale, like a kill, may require a ruthless streak that runs counter to the traditional image of the nurturant women. On the other hand, nurturance and the careful tending and service of customers, like the careful tending of crops, clearly contribute to success in building long-term customer relationships.

If athletics, especially team sports, are evolved training for hunters and warriors, then the increasing involvement of girls and women in these activities may be helping to prepare them for corporate roles in sales and manufacturing. But those who are most successful in developing traits of dominance and competitiveness, as well as those who train their bodies for strength and endurance, may be unwittingly sacrificing biological advantages in areas of nurturance and child rearing. Studies of female professional athletes suggest that those who work out to remain in top physical condition may undergo hormonal changes that result in smaller breasts and irregular menstrual cycles. As they become warriors, they may also secrete more androgen, less estrogen, and seek in their sexual encounters to adopt a more dominant role. Perhaps it is not that surprising that some top female athletes get involved in homosexual relationships.

Recognizing the archetypal differences in the roles of hunters and gatherers may also explain why women seem to find less resistance when pursuing corporate careers in staff, as opposed to line management roles. The hunter's independence and ruthless streak may be less important in accounting, personnel, legal departments and data processing. The nurturance of women may represent an asset in teaching, customer services and personnel administration.

The fact that much more has been written about hunting and man's aggressive nature than about gathering may represent another example of chauvinistic blindness. We have become conditioned to think of men as the "breadwinners", the providers. Early men have been described many times as pack-hunting predators. Yet this label only applied to the males. It is important to recognize that women have always played a major role in providing food. As agriculture emerged, the gathering tasks of women evolved from searching for wild edible food to the more patient tasks of planting, tending and nurturing crops and raising domestic animals. The pattern of women staying nearer the home camp and covering less territory on a daily basis continued. The image of the farmer's wife tending the vegetable garden, milking the cows, gathering eggs and assisting with planting and harvesting is a common one. And it demonstrates that during the age of agriculture, women continued to be responsible for a major portion of the food supply.

It might be argued that in the early stages of industrialization when workers began to migrate from the cropland to cities in large numbers, women, perhaps for the first time in anthropological history, lost their role as major food providers. Men were first to be absorbed into the new industrial tribes. From this perspective, the phenomena of large numbers of women joining corporate tribes may be seen as correcting a temporary imbalance.

Research on the male role among animals, as it relates to claiming and defending territory, may be important for female executives to understand, because it involves the competition for office space. As described in Chapter Two, the powerful drive to capture and defend territory operates on several levels. Men are still called upon to fight, kill and die for the territory of their nation-state. Within a nation-state they compete in less bloody ways for real estate. Sports such as football, hockey, basketball, soccer and rugby involve a ritual struggle for territory. Corporations continually wage bloodless wars to capture market share within defined territories.

On another level, the competition for an office near the president on "executive row" is a dynamic, ongoing process. If the struggle for territorial control is primarily a male preoccupation, as it appears to be with many species, female executives may be at a disadvantage. Corporations are careful about allotting office space. Moving up to a larger office is usually a clear sign of advancement in the corporate pecking order. Are women managers less driven than men to expand their office space? Are they less successful than men in claiming prime space for their departments during budget negotiations or office relocations?

In many species, some of the most fierce and aggressive behavior is displayed by females. But it is normally elicited in the defense of young. The circumference of their territorial defense may be smaller than that of males. It appears to be focused on the nest.

In the past three decades the flow of women into corporate tribes has increased so dramatically that 54% of working-age females in the U.S. are now earning paychecks. Technology is an essential reason for this, because machines eliminate the importance of differences in physical strength.

As skill at making a profit increasingly replaces military power as the primary survival challenge for modern tribes, as world trade increases and corporations continue to replace hunting and farming activities in the third world, opportunities for influencing changes in male and female roles will continue to increase.

The same forces which liberated workers from hard labor, which made dramatic inroads against poverty and which launched the new age of corporate tribes, also lifted the burden of hard labor from women.

Machines have largely eliminated the more obvious reasons for dividing work into sex groups. But progress for women in penetrating the leadership and councils of elders of corporations may depend on a more clear understanding of male and female bonding, of the evolved hunting-gathering and war activities of corporations, of the succession process, and of competition within the pecking order.

In spite of our growing understanding of how male and female roles develop, all modern corporations and governments—like the tribes before them—are male dominated. The higher up in the pecking order one looks, the fewer women can be found.

Studies of male and female bonding may help us to better understand why this is so, and what pitfalls lie ahead in our attempts to modify traditional male and female roles.

The Chief

The modern counterparts of hunting and gathering roles are sometimes obscure, but the position at the top of the pyramid is easily recognized.

Wherever there is a pecking order, there is a head pecker. He is alpha, the chief, the dominant male. This most visible role exists in all higher animals. Alpha is usually a large, powerful male, in good health. But he is not always the largest and strongest. He often extends his reign past his prime of physical strength by bluff, reputation, the psychological advantage of being in control of prime territory or by having defeated rivals in the past. Baboon chiefs get assistance from loyal lieutenants when a serious challenge emerges from the ranks. Thus, a cooperative group of mature males teams up to maintain control over the pack.

Among many species, including walruses, elephants, baboons and gorillas, alpha displays his leadership in situations of attack and defense. It is the dominant male in the elephant herd who rushes the threatening cameraman. It is the dominant male baboon who must strike out alone to search for and locate predatory leopards when they threaten the troop. And it is the dominant gorilla who hoots, hollers and beats his chest in a convincing blast of anger and power when his group is threatened.

When the walrus colony is attacked, the dominant male is last to retreat. He provides protection to the colony by threatening attackers while the others escape. Subordinate males are often encouraged by the dominant male and will return, after their initial flight, to stand behind him.

Among humans, the notion that the captain goes down with the ship presents compelling parallels.

The dominant male often eats first. Even among lions, the dominant male, who is too large and slow to be an effective hunter, is the first to eat his fill from a fresh kill.

In mammals, the dominant male often displays a more active sex life than the other males. In many species he maintains the largest harem and contributes more than his fair share of offspring to the succeeding generation. Relatively recent research results suggest he may also kill or drive off young males of his own species who might become competitors for territory or females. The examples of sending young men off to war, of quarrels that erupt between fathers and their teenage sons, or the firing of brash junior executives who push too hard may all be rooted in our mammalian ancestry.

The dominant male commands prime territory. He is found in the best breeding area, the best shelter, the best perch, the best position in the pack. And a dominant male in control of a prime patch of territory has a psychological advantage over competitors.

The evolving role of the dominant male follows the same time frame and territorial sequences described earlier. So, as man's survival activities changed, first from hunting and gathering to agriculture, and then from agriculture to corporate activities, new knowledge and skills were required for leadership. Following is an examination of these changes.

Alpha in Hunting-Gathering Tribes

The first chiefs of human tribes were skilled hunters and warriors. Physical strength and intelligence were essential to leadership. Where skill at hunting was important for survival, the man who excelled gained prestige and recognition from other tribesmen. A man who was unable to provide for his own family was regarded as a liability within hunting tribes. The hunter who bagged more than his family needed was clearly an asset. He commanded respect. Others were willing to follow him and he rose to positions of influence. Among the Bedouin tribes, visitors reported as late as the 1800s that the fiercest, strongest and craftiest obtained complete mastery over his fellows.[41]

Chiefs of many hunting-gathering tribes were thought to have supernatural powers. The god-chief phenomenon was widespread in primitive tribes throughout the world. The chief was "hot," spiritually. In *Totem and Taboo*, Freud[42] indicates that rulers were "vehicles of the mysterious and dangerous magical power which is transmitted by contact like an electric charge and which brings death and ruin to anyone who is not protected by a similar charge".

Many taboos surrounded the early tribal head men. Some could not be touched. They often had special diets. They were war lords and judges, loved and hated, valued and feared. Some became so highly insulated and controlled by ceremonies and rituals which evolved around them that they could hardly function.

Their skills at hunting and war were intimately intertwined with the environment which supported them. Magic was and is a major element in the daily life of primitive tribes. And the one who could explain and ease the fears of dangerous and uncontrollable events — this man assumed immense power.

When his power failed, a chief was often killed. When his powers could not provide sufficient food for the tribe or protection from witchcraft, diseases, the elements or enemies, tribesmen tended to lose faith in their leader and often voted him out with violence and bloodshed. Unusual risks, as well as benefits, are associated with the top of the pyramid.

Most so-called primitive tribes, influenced by their contact with modern men, are in a stage of rapid transition. Old leaders are losing credibility. New ones, whose skills are more similar to those of corporate tribesmen, are emerging.

★   ★   ★

Until modern man recently changed the rules, Wukahupi tribesmen of Western New Guinea engaged in continual blood feuds with neighboring tribes. Like the vendettas of the Mafia, and the feuds of the Tennessee hill country, men of the Wukahupi tribes engaged in an ongoing competition for human lives. When one tribe led a successful raid, one that resulted in a kill, the tribe of the victim became motivated to even the score.

Season after season the process repeated itself, with each tribe planning raids or luring enemy raiders into traps. The threat of raids was ever present. So much so, that high lookout towers were built near the fields where women planted and harvested yams. In spite of meticulous caution and watchfulness, the killing continued. When one tribe effected a kill, cries of victory and mourning echoed over the land, and tribesmen marked off the score in their minds.

The competition for kills was an integral part of the Wukahupi tribesman's daily life. The man with skulls displayed in his hut gained influence and prestige in the eyes of his peers. The tasks of the tribe clearly favored men with skills in killing and evading attack.

The introduction of rifles among some headhunting tribes had such a grisly result that something had to change. With bow and arrow and spear, the competition between warriors of neighboring tribes had retained an acceptable balance of deaths. But a small group of headhunters, armed with rifles, could and did wipe out entire villages with very little difficulty.

This sudden escalation overthrew the balances that had become established. Responding, the government of New Guinea passed and enforced laws against headhunting, and these laws have had a major impact on the tribes, the fabric of their daily life, the pecking orders, interpersonal relationships and the process of ascendancy to leadership. By imposing a foreign value system on the tribesmen, the government "contaminated" the culture.

For the Wukahupi tribesmen, the government rulings created a shift from skill at hunting to a skill in commerce and economics. The new leader is one who can host a large pig feast. The larger the feast, the more prestige is gained by the host.

Acquiring pigs takes a different set of skills than stalking and spearing enemy tribesmen. In many respects, these skills are similar to those required to make a profit. First, the New Guinea tribeman must build capital. To do this, he goes to a sort of pig banker and agrees to raise a litter (feed is a major cost item) in exchange for one of the pigs. The seasoned pig banker may farm out many litters, and in this way build his holdings dramatically. At the same time he passes his feed costs on to the man who is trying to get started.

A pig feast, like a Cadillac or a yacht, is a display of wealth. And the acquisition of wealth is an objective which both the Wukahupi and the modern corporate tribesman understands. The new and future chiefs of the Wukahupi may have skills which are more similar to those of corporate presidents than to warriors.

The Chief in Agricultural Tribes

When tribes evolved from hunting to agriculture, from aggressive, predatory methods for acquiring food to raising animals or crops, the constellation of skills and knowledge required for leadership changed dramatically.

During the agricultural revolution, predatory hunting skills were refocused on the task of acquiring and controlling food-producing territory. And the best real estate men in the agricultural age were generals. They made very large real estate deals without the aid of attorneys. They used armies. They also collected slaves, sheep and cattle from conquered tribes, as well as taxes. Predatory behavior, first with hordes and later with trained and equipped armies on a massive scale, is characteristic of the agricultural age.

Customs regarding inheritance were blended into the recipe for leadership for men of all cultures and ages, but it took on immense significance as agriculture emerged. Land ownership and control meant power. Leadership was related to control of territory, and when property and leadership was passed from father to son, family dynasties emerged. Family governments also grew, became more stable and more complex.

The transition from hunting and gathering to agriculture had the effect of increasing tribal size, generating food surpluses and immense wealth. This wealth and power were blended with the ruler's magic and divinity. One result was that the god-chiefs became god-kings.

God-kings have ruled billions of our ancestors. In tribes all over the earth, men have believed that alpha was superhuman. He was god, or god's child, or especially favored by god. Most god-kings were taught from infancy that they were divine, by sincere teachers who believed it themselves. Divine rulers have existed in China, Tahiti, ancient Peru under the Incas, Egypt, among the king-prophets of the Hebrews, in Japan, Africa, Scandinavia, Italy and Tibet. Crazy Horse, the famous war chief of the Sioux, was a relatively recent example. A clearer translation of this Indian name may be Enchanted, or Magic Horse. He was believed to be, like Achilles, protected from arrows in battle by a magic force.

Japan and China were ruled by god-kings up to and during World War II. Haile Selassie, the combined god and leader of Ethiopia, is a recent example. So was the Dalai Lama of Tibet and the Shah of Iran. Jimmy Carter had a certain god-man luster. Ronald Reagan seems to have very little doubt that God is on his side.

The Chief in Corporate Tribes

The position of president is still a focal point for tribal attention with obvious benefits of territory, pay, influence and power. It exerts a magnetic pull to all ambitious executives.

In addition to the financial rewards of being the top man in a tribe, there are also powerful emotional rewards. Many men hunger for the power, the prestige, and the independence they feel the chief role provides. Many are surprised to discover that the position of president is not that different from other executive positions. The power and independence are often illusory. The president must still satisfy the chairman of the board and the council of elders. He may find it is as difficult to implement his ideas as it was to get his programs approved from above when he was a director or vice president.

Selection of alpha, and identification of characteristics which lead to ascendancy and leadership, represent a prime area of interest and research among industrial psychologists.

Research on birth order shows that many presidents are eldest sons. The same research points out that eldest children are significantly higher achievers than later born siblings. First-born children usually benefit from richer interaction with adults. They gain slightly higher intelligence test scores.

My own observations of the personality characteristics of corporate presidents suggests that they are energetic and socially skilled individuals who fill their daily lives with activities. They appear to meet more people, read more, travel more and sleep less than lower level executives. Although they are not particularly intellectual in their tastes, they gain higher intelligence test scores, on the average, than lower-level executives.

McClelland[43] has indicated they may also have stronger power drives, more achievement motivation, and a ruthless streak. Further research is needed to determine if, like earlier chiefs, they have more active sex lives than other men or contribute more than their share of genes to the succeeding generation. Research has confirmed that tall men are promoted more frequently and get better performance evaluations than shorter men, so size counts. But corporate presidents come in a wide variery of shapes and sizes. They are clearly not the largest and strongest hunters and warriors.

Corporate presidents I have known, often reveal leadership early in life. They are captain of the football team, president of their high school or the youngest manager in the division. They also become financially independent from parents and begin to earn their own money earlier than their age mates.

In 1975, I completed a longitudinal study of the management of a major transportation corporation. I had been testing outside candidates, acting as a quality-control screen for newly hired executives for about ten years. In that time, I had administered a battery of intelligence and personality tests to 119 candidates for various middle and upper-management positions.

Over the years, many of those hired had quickly risen to leadership positions. Others had risen more slowly. Several had left as a result of conflict, impatience or mutual dissatisfaction. To obtain management norms, we compiled test results from the California Personality Inventory, and four measures of intellectual skill. We also studied results of several sub-groups, including those who had the highest salary-to-age ratios and those who had, for one reason or another, left the organization.

In the corporate tribe, as well as its predecessor tribes, there is a clear correlation between age and position in the pecking order. A pattern emerges which roughly separates men into age levels. For this reason, the ratio of a man's salary to his age is a key to his ascendancy in the pecking order. A ratio of 1.00 means he is earning $20,000 by age 20, $30,000 by age 30, $40,000 by age 40, etc.

The transportation corporation client's highest salary-to-age ratio employees were clearly in leadership positions. One of them would very likely rise to the alpha position in the normal process of management succession.

We calculated separate means for these sub-groups, then ran the whole thing through a computer to identify significant differences in group means.

Our findings revealed, perhaps predictably, that high salary-to-age ratio managers differed significantly from the management norms on several personality measures. Essentially, they were more dominant, more self-confident and more tolerant than those with lower salary-to-age ratios. They also had above-average scores in areas of achievement drive. They wanted badly to succeed, to win.

But the high-turnover group provided a few surprises. They were also more dominant and self-confident than other managers, but scores in areas of maturity and socialization were significantly lower. We were surprised to note that those who left the organization had a slight edge in intelligence over those who remained with the corporation. It is well known that highly intelligent clerical workers turn over more rapidly than others. Our results indicated that the principle may also apply at management levels.

We interpreted these results as indicating that there were some intelligent, impatient, and dominant individuals who were also more independent, less loyal, less mature, and less committed to the corporation than other managers. They may have seen the corporation as a stepping-stone in their careers. They tended to become bored and impatient after a few years, particularly if their duties became repetitive. They often made creative contributions, but they also represented higher turnover risks. Some felt uncomfortable with the conformity required, or the atmosphere of authority and control that cramped their style.

In a sense, these men may be part of a normal pattern of tribesmen searching for their places in a tribe, confronting those above them and losing internal battles for dominance. Often they leave to start their own tribes. Many firings within corporations are the result of normal struggles for dominance. As with other mammals, Homo-sapiens may run off competitors who are so aggressive, independent or intelligent that they threaten those in power.

Leaders of corporations with many profit centers can reduce the risk of picking the wrong leaders by observing the track records of executives as they graduate through increasing levels of line or staff responsibility. Boards of conglomerates have the advantage of long periods of measured financial results to guide their promotion judgments.

The Passing of the God-Kings

Corporate presidents have largely abandoned the ages old delusion of grandeur regarding their own divinity. But the general deterioration of divine or supernatural powers in the chief is a relatively recent event. It parallels the emergence of science. But elements of it remain in the exaggerated fear and adoration that employees hold for their top man. Employees build legends about their top men. They admire and fear them, often yielding a deference, different only in degree, from that given the god-kings of the agricultural age.

Although few corporate presidents claim to have divine or supernatural powers, employees often seem to respond to them as though they were "hot" with special powers. The president gets on the elevator with a new secretary, and her heart pounds madly. She is terrified when he says "good morning".

In his daydreams of meeting with the president, the young executive composes grand speeches. But when the moment arrives his eloquent fantasy evaporates. He finds himself saying inane things. Because of the aura of power, he is unnerved by exposure to alpha. So, employees often react to their president with traces of the same feelings of fear, awe and trepidation that earlier tribesmen felt toward their god-chiefs. When the president takes the floor, futher discussion is often in poor taste. Many top leaders are largely unaware of the butterflies they stir up in employees' stomachs. But many employees are mesmerized, frozen by the power, prestige and reputation of their tribal leaders.

Although alpha attracts a sort of primal fascination from tribesmen, corporations are really run by teams. In most modern corporations, there is a core group of top men who call the shots. They compete with one another but they also protect one another. Admission to the leadership core group usually requires approval of the council of elders. That approval usually means they have developed a sense of respect for the executive's capabilities.

As the survival challenges evolved, first from hunting to agriculture, and in the last 100 years, from agriculture to industry, the natural selection process for the tribal chief has also evolved. The first major shift was from skill at hunting, to skill at the capture, control and production of food-growing territory. The most recent shift has been from skill at controlling territory and agriculture, to skill at leading a corporation. It involves a basic knowledge of business administration, finance, accounting, marketing, production, human resources, planning and of executing plans.

To make a profit, to increase earnings and enhance the value of the stock, increase tribal growth — these are the key qualities currently in use for selecting a new president.

Although the precise formula for becoming the chief and mastering the skills required for rising to the top will remain a focus of research for years to come, the chief and his archetypal role at the top of the tribal pyramid is, and has been, an essential facet in the life and experience of tribal people for millions of years.

Councils of Elders

Almost all modern corporations have a board of directors. Most really don't know why. Is it a custom? A legal necessity? A corporate policy? Studies of tribes suggest that similar governing bodies of older men exist in tribes all over the world. The council of elders provided review of decisions and rendered policy judgments on critical tribal matters among the Sioux Indians. Among the Yomba of Nigeria, the king's power was counterbalanced by a council of elders who could cause him to be deposed or even executed for malperformance. The South Nias Islanders of Indonesia functioned with two groups of elders who faced one another during ceremonies and divided their responsibilities according to tradition. The right-hand elders, who formed the clan of the upper world, faced elders of the left-hand clan, who officiated at funeral rites and ceremonies having to do with the dead.

Conflicts within the Small Nambas tribes of Malekula Island in the New Hebrides were settled by a jury of elders. Trials were presided over by a chief, who received advice from each of the elders individually before rendering a verdict.

It is doubtful that the modern board of directors recognizes that the board room is an evolved council hut. Neither do they understand that their role is an ancient one, one that may have substantial survival value for the tribes they help govern.

In 1964, Amacom made a comprehensive study of boards of directors. In *The Corporate Directorship*, its authors provide solid data on these modern councils of elders. They vary in size according to the size of the corporation, ranging from a median of five for organizations under five million in annual sales, to fourteen in corporations which have annual sales of over a billion. In banks, these councils are somewhat larger.

> *"The common practice is for directors to be elected annually . . . Frequently, a corporate director, when elected, continues in office for the duration of his business life or longer, even though he may be subject to annual reelection."*

Duties of the modern board of directors often include:

> *"Electing the Chief Executive Officer and the other officers of the company . . . Appraising the performance of the officers and fixing their compensation."*[44]

Most boards also have the power to replace the president.

These boards are made up primarily of older men. The most common retirement age is 70, although at least 30% stay until age 72. Since 60 or 65 is the normal retirement age for other employees, it is clear that boards are literally made up of elders.

Directors have periodic board meetings during the year. Most companies have four to six meetings per year.

These top level, mostly male clusters, often combine both inside and outside executives. The outside executives get paid per meeting, usually a modest amount, to cover travel expenses.

Relationships within the board vary with each tribe. I have worked with boards made up of closely knit family members, with sleepy old codgers at the edge of senility who embarrassed everyone by dozing off, with gracious and seasoned corporate leaders who had proven their skills in leading other companies, and with boards which were deeply involved with the day-to-day operations of their companies. I have observed top executives in the creation of new boards, and helped in carefully selecting new board members who would assist in achieving corporate objectives.

In all these cases, the council of elders represents the uppermost slice of age stratification. Boards of directors, like other councils of elders, embody the oldest and, theoretically, wisest strata. Since they have long since proven their capability to contribute to tribal survival and growth, they are often able to ameliorate the ambitious and occasionally egocentric striving for growth and profits that are often characteristic of men in their 30s and 40s. The council of elders often sees broader issues—long range growth, the health of the tribe as a whole, community responsibility, and broad national and international issues—more clearly than men on the firing line who are actively involved in the daily struggle for the tribe's survival and growth.

The board plays, perhaps it has always played, a key role in tribal man's survival. It contributes experience, knowledge and leadership, as well as "being cognizant of the interests of the company as a whole."[45]

Councils of elders in hunter-gatherer tribes and in agricultural tribes were key participants in ceremonies, religious rituals, and group tribal events.

The magic, supernatural, and mystical functions which earlier councils of elders believed in have largely disappeared from the board rooms of the corporate tribes. One occasionally encounters an opening prayer, but most meetings involve rather calm, congenial, businesslike interactions, which are devoid of spiritual or religious content.

Like the president, the board of the modern corporation is evolving away from claims of divine influence.

The Headshrinker

I was driving home from an executive development seminar, completely drained. For a week I had been leading intensive simulation exercises, specifically designed to develop and assess managerial skill. I had observed six hand-picked executives as they led meetings, planned projects, gave presentations and conducted competitive negotiations. I had also analyzed samples of their administrative work to assess their skills at delegating, decision making, planning, public relations and employee relations.

After each of these simulation exercises, I had led a peer feedback session.

It had been an excellent group. They had been both sincere and constructive with one another, sharing their ideas on how each could further strengthen his management skill and effectiveness.

Still, I was tuckered out. The emotional pitch and tension of the sessions, especially during the peer feedback episodes, was exhausting.

As I cruised over the Gray's Bay bridge between Wayzata and Deephaven, Minnesota, I recalled how the vice president of sales had been shocked by the peer feedback following his leadership exercise. He had blown it. He had obviously made up his mind about the solution before the meeting started. Rather than give his staff an opportunity to influence his decision or contribute ideas, he had treated them as peons. He began the exercise with a long, heavy-handed statement of the problem. Then he gave them his solution, made assignments, and closed the exercise well ahead of his time limit. Several of his key staff never opened their mouths. He had been all-powerful.

During the peer feedback session, the peer group had told him how they felt about his management style. He was surprised. He had always been proud of his booming command presence. But he was insensitive to the demeaning impact his style had on others.

The peer feedback plunged him into a thoughtful reassessment. By the end of the week he had clearly modified his bombastic behavior. He was listening.

The next day, in one of life's amazing coincidences, my research into tribology led me to discover another peer feedback session, deep in the jungles of the upper Amazon.[46]

> For several days, Xuri Kaya (Colored Bird) had returned from the hunt empty handed. He told many stories about his bad luck, but he also felt terrible. "My family is being fed by others, which brings me great shame and leaves me with

obligations that I will never be able to pay off unless my luck changes."

Xumu, the shaman, called the men together. The hunters gathered to sit around the fire, and the palaver went on for half the night.

Xuri Kaya brought all of his hunting gear; snares made of strong twine treated with beeswax, a large open basket of palm fronds used to catch small jungle partridges that sleep together on the ground at night, several lances, a large bow, a dozen arrows, and his bamboo knife. He meticulously reviewed his hunting methods, plans, and strategies with his peers. They questioned him carefully.

Then, each man, in turn, gave sincere and thoughtful feedback. The snares had not been properly treated with herbs to remove the smell of man. The lances had been affected by iuxibo (evil spirits). Each was trying to help Xuri Kaya to be a more successful and effective hunter. Each knew that his improvement would benefit the entire tribe.

Until that insightful moment, I had thought peer feedback for purposes of strengthening performance was a new and innovative technique. It clearly was not. There it was, faithfully recorded in the writings of Manuel Cordova Rios. Peer feedback is ancient—tried and true.

It also became clearer to me that my own role, as an outside consulting psychologist, was an ancient one.

In tribes throughout the world, widely separated by oceans, jungles, mountains and deserts, anthropologists have observed a perplexing phenomenon. Certain tribesmen gain influence and status within the tribe by virtue of some kind of special knowledge. These "men-of-knowledge"[47] are known by a variety of names. They are the wise men, priests, warlocks, shaman, medicine men, brujos, fetishers, prophets, soothsayers, wizards and witch doctors. Some were astronomers, others alchemists or medical practitioners. Some studied herbs and potions, some math, astronomy and geometry.

Many were merely scholars, seekers of knowledge who operated in homemade laboratories and struggled for truth without the aid of libraries. Their fellow tribesmen often regarded them with suspicion, fear or awe. Early medical practitioners who dissected cadavers were regarded as ghouls by the uneducated common man. Some made truly remarkable discoveries, especially considering that they studied without the aid of books, microscopes, chemistry or electricity.

Man's concepts of God and Satan, heaven and hell, evolve and change over the ages, just as other aspects of the tribe evolve. And the man-of-knowledge evolved along with everything else. Those who rise to the top of their special pyramids are men who can provide the most acceptable explanation of important but uncertain events. Those who can produce the most convincing miracles—feats of knowledge and power—also gain credibility.

Moses is a classic example of the tribal man-of-knowledge. Archimedes, Aristotle, Faust, Merlin, Joseph, Rasputin, the Dalai Lama and the Pope all fit the archetypical image of tribal shamen. Because they were thought to have special knowledge, they were asked for answers to the difficult questions which faced the tribe. Questions like: "What happens to us when we die?", and "Where does the lightning and thunder come from?"

These wise men or priests officiated at ceremonies and became keepers and interpreters of tribal and religious traditions. They also served as intermediaries with gods and spirits.

Freud believed that all the thousands of tribal explanations of the world, all the stories passed on by elders, wise men and priests, could be categorized into three groups: animism, religion, and science.[48] I believe these three traditions for explaining the world correspond to the ages of hunting-gathering, agriculture and technology.

> Hunter-gatherer—Explanations of the world about them are animistic. Some totem groups believe they literally descended from animals. Their world is crowded with spirits— wind spirits, volcano gods, thunder spirits, spirits in animals, in trees and vegetables. They fear sorcery and magic.

Agriculture—Rain gods, fertility gods, gods of rice, grain and corn emerge. Tribes are led by god-kings. The spirits have evolved into mostly human forms. The gods are human. There are large, religious organizations, large worshipping houses, elaborate ceremonies, complex political organizations. Their armies fight for God and country.

Technology—Corporations emerge. Technology emerges. Men turn to science for explanations of the world.

Berelson and Steiner indicate that "religious belief and practice is most likely to be brought into play by individuals and societies in connection with important but uncertain matters (e.g. birth and death, war, accidents, danger, etc.)."

They quote Malinowski's studies of the Trobriand Islanders:[49]

> *"While in the villages on the inner lagoon fishing is done in an easy and absolutely reliable manner by the method of poisoning, yielding abundant results without danger and uncertainty, there are on the shores of the open sea dangerous modes of fishing and also certain types in which the yield greatly varies according to whether shoals of fish appear beforehand or not. It is most significant that in the lagoon fishing, where man can rely completely upon his knowledge and skill, magic does not exist, while in the open-sea fishing, full of danger and uncertainty, there is extensive magical ritual to secure safety and good results."*

Men of knowledge allayed tensions and fears by offering explanations and providing ceremonial remedies in response to uncontrollable events, particularly dangerous ones. They attempted to explain and control illness, disease, the weather, death, fertility, the harvest, fortunes of war and the hunt.

A friend of mine served a two-and-a-half-year stint with the Peace Corps in Togo.

His job was digging wells for villages. Whenever he would enter a new village, a brief ceremony would take place. A chicken would be killed, sometimes several. After the appropriate introductions he would pose a question to the chief: "Would you like us to drill a well in the center of your village?"

The issue would rattle through the village with hundreds of discussions and opinions—the chief getting advice from all sides—and, finally came the answer. "Yes, we would like a well."

In those discussions the women would tip the scales in favor of the well almost every time. The well would liberate them from centuries of carrying water balanced on their heads, in tremendous jars, several hundred yards daily between the village and the nearest stream.

One day a quarrel erupted in the village. One woman accused another of witchcraft. The entire village was on edge as the quarrel raged. Finally, the fetisher was called in.

Who is the fetisher? No one wins against the fetisher. His power is supreme. He is the traveling super witch doctor, priest, wizard.

The fetisher arrived and conducted a ceremony that confirmed the accusation that the woman was indeed a witch. Then the fetisher cast out the evil and cured the woman of her witchcraft. Having solved an immense problem for the entire village, he went on to his next assignment.

Similar encounters occur frequently within corporate tribes, as the following story demonstrates.

   ★   ★   ★

Barney Hansen is a fictitious name, but he was Barney-like—large and roly-poly, an awkward bear. He was an accountant in XYZ's corporate accounting organization.

Barney got on the elevator, as always, at 8:00 a.m. He was a bit annoyed when it stopped at the second floor. An attractive female office clerk got on the elevator. She held some large computer tab runs in her arms.

There they were, breasts, unfettered by a brassiere, with thinly covered nipples on a platter of computer printouts.

Zow! A fuse blew in Barney's mind. Barney reached out and tweaked one helpless nipple there in the elevator.

The girl reported to her supervisor in tears, and the crunching machinery of the corporate disciplinary procedures began to turn.

The news was passed directly to the boss, then boss-to-boss the spark leaped to the top. Then to the vice president of personnel. Corporate information travels like a neural impulse from the receptor at the point of stimulation, through the main information channels to the brains, where it is weighed, judged and delegated to the appropriate department for action.

The vice president of personnel contacted a local head-shrinker. What shall we do? Is he crazy? Is he a pervert?

The headshrinker asks, "Has there been any recent change in his behavior?"

Personnel V.P.: "I don't think so."

"Does he appear to be friendly? Does he have friends—does he have lunch alone? Does he seem flat, depressed or unhappy?"

The shaman was probing for evidence of the demon schizophrenia. Classical symptoms include bizarre behavior, interpersonal aversiveness, and adhedonia (loss of pleasure with life).

Personnel V.P.: "He is married, two children, good work record. Good sense of humor."

Barney arrived promptly at his meeting with the shrink. He seemed embarrassed by all the attention he was getting. So he had tweaked her nipple—was that such a crime? He was sorry. He certainly would not do it again.

Tests confirmed a certain awkwardness in social situations, but there was no evidence of serious emotional problems. In fact, Barney seemed healthy, happily married and well adjusted.

Barney was told clearly that "Yes, it is definitely a crime," and "if the girl wished to press charges the company would support her". Barney was given an official reprimand and told to keep his hands to himself.

Barney had broken a tribal rule and had been officially

punished. He had also been sent to an evolved headshrinker who had searched for, but this time had not found any demons.

★   ★   ★

When two tribes or cultures meet, there is often a mixing of belief systems, as well as a competition by the men-of-knowledge for the belief of the tribesmen. When tribes are defeated or fail to survive, the gods of their tribe and their tribal definitions of the universe, heaven, hell, etc., also suffer. Conversely, the gods of strong and growing tribes gain strength. They attract new believers.

As agents for spreading European tribal beliefs of the 1700 and 1800s, the Christian missionaries are unparalleled. Following in the wake of conquerors and explorers, they can take credit for destroying and distorting thousands of competing beliefs, traditions, religions and cultures. In their place, they installed the belief system of the Judeo-Christian tradition which happened to be in vogue back home in the conquering nations of Europe.

The earliest tribal accounts on record were provided by missionaries. So they must be read with an attempt to understand the writer's belief system, his moral judgment of the events and behavior he observed, and the impact his presence may have had on the events as he observed them.

In his studies of Easter Island, Francis Maziere[50] indicates that the tribal dances were among the first aspects of the native culture to perish. Essentially, the sexual taboos of the missionaries' tribe were imposed on the dancers. The dancers were made to feel ashamed of their nakedness and the sexual aspects of their ceremony. Missionaries probably considered it a great victory when their influence could be strong enough so that the dances were no longer practiced.

When these aspects of tribal worship and culture perished on Easter Island, missionaries introduced new rituals, new ceremonies, new values and new sets of taboos. The dances were lost forever. Only a few references to them remain in ships' logs and cave drawings. Certainly, no decent missionary would commit such pornography to writing.

As with all other tribes, American Indians had their own ideas about nudity and modesty. Family members often went naked in their hogans and bathed without shame in nearby rivers, even in the dead of winter. From under their multiple layers of heavy clothing and Victorian taboos, early European settlers regarded such behavior as barbarian.

The cross-fertilization that takes place when two cultures interact takes some interesting turns. The voodoo and witchcraft practices of Caribbean and imported African tribes, when blended with Christian theology, create a fascinating array of hybrid belief systems. Satan becomes the evil jungle god— rolled into one, complex image.

Mormon missionaries who baptized hundreds of Samoans into their church in the early 1900s were continually upset when their new members, who seemed devoted in every way to Mormonism, still carried out many of the ceremonies of their native religion. The Samoans seemed unperturbed by the apparent conflicts in serving Christ as well as their god of the sea.

There is ample evidence that tribal gods do wane. No one knows how many humans were tossed into Hawaiian volcanoes to appease the gods. If the gods who used to inhabit the volcanoes of Hawaii are not dead, they are clearly less feared. They faded with the Hawaiians who believed in them.

Tribes create their after-life concepts out of familiar objects and surroundings. The Greeks believed Mount Olympus was a holy place. Heaven, for the American Plains Indians, was a happy hunting ground with plenty of buffalo. One South Sea island tribe placed its dead in canoes decorated with flowers and cast them adrift. The current would carry the dead to heaven—over the western horizon where the sun sank into the sea.

The acceptance of European religions by more primitive tribes in various parts of the world parallels an erosion of power and credibility of local shamen and witch doctors. Significantly, it also undermined local beliefs regarding the chief's divinity. Every missionary knows there is only one god—the one his tribesmen back home in Europe and America believe in. So missionaries often found themselves in direct competition with the god-kings.

Like Moses, they competed with the local wizards, and they usually won. Their knowledge, represented by their machines, rifles, metal knives, outboard engines, drugs and medicines, electric generators, cameras and cigarette lighters, gave them more control of their environments, more security from the unknown, more magic and power than the shaman could muster.

★   ★   ★

Modern technology has dealt some fatal blows to tribal gods and religious traditions. When the Zambezi River was dammed, some Kalihari tribesmen who had inhabited the land that was to be inundated faced doom. Their land, their homes, their sacred places and hunting grounds would soon be covered with hundreds of feet of water.

When government representatives met with the tribal leaders to explain the situation, the Kalihari could not bring themselves to believe the strange story. The idea that the land they had loved, hunted and buried their ancestors in since the beginning of time would be covered with water seemed absurd. The Kalihari called upon their men-of-knowledge for guidance.

The Kalihari believe that certain gigantic trees in their region are holy. And their medicine men, with much fasting, prayer and ceremonial tradition, went to the trees, seeking guidance and inspiration. Finally, the holy men returned to the elders with an answer. The Kalihari should not abandon their homes and hunting grounds.

In the end, as the water slowly swallowed the land, the

Kalihari yielded to the potent medicine of the machine men.
The holy trees, which had guided the tribes through generations, were last to sink beneath the rising surface of the
lake.

★   ★   ★

Just as technology has destroyed tribal gods throughout the
world, so also has it eroded some of the credibility of traditional
beliefs regarding God and heaven among modern men.

Concepts of God and heaven have evolved into amorphous,
abstract, spiritual things. God can no longer be located geo-
graphically. God is now perceived by many as a spirit, a law
of nature, a coordinating force.

The role of the corporate man-of-knowledge has also
changed. No longer is he a priest, a god man or a spiritual
intermediary. Now his special knowledge comes from science.

Einstein's medicine was more powerful, more convincing,
more miraculous than that of the religious or spiritual man-of-
knowledge. From his scraggly head came the largest explosions
man had ever known—nuclear bombs. There is little doubt
that the bomb has had profound influence on the thinking of
all modern men. We need no longer fear the volcano god. But
the bomb is a new fear. All men must reckon with it.

Landing men on the moon is another miraculous feat. It
draws man's admiration to science, away from the miracles of
organized religion.

The influence of the modern man-of-knowledge can be immense. The research scientists who perfected the birth control
pill earned millions for G. D. Searle and Company in Chicago.
They also changed the sexual habits of modern man, helped
liberate modern woman, and gave the foundations of Catholicism a hearty shake. They also may have saved mankind from
overpopulation.

When man landed on the moon, when photographs of the
surface of Mars were published, traditional concepts of heaven
were undermined.

As a child, the medicine-men of my tribe gave me a reasonably well-constructed concept of heaven. It was a beautiful place. There was no death or disease. I would see my relatives. Those who died before me would greet me and rejoice with me when I arrived. God would be there. Somehow, I got the feeling that heaven was up in the sky. Perhaps on a distant star.

We found out a few years ago that heaven was not on the moon. Photographs from Mars reveal no golden gates. I really don't expect the first spacemen on Venus to meet my grandfather, waiting there. Where is heaven, really? What has become of it?

Modern man worships science. We are astounded by the miracles science can produce. Scientists are convincing when they fly men to the moon. Their magic is stronger, more impressive, than that of religious men-of-knowledge. Science has become like God to us and may, in fact, be largely responsible for the "God is dead" feelings that have been plaguing organized religions of our time. Science produces miracles, and miracles have always impressed the masses.

Modern business corporations hire scientists, attorneys, computer experts, Ph.D. researchers, geologists, psychologists, operations research analysts, financial analysts, engineers, futurists and market analysts with their amazing statistical tools. These are the wise men, wizards, soothsayers, headshrinkers, brujos, prophets, and witch doctors of the corporate tribe. Sometimes it seems that modern corporations are waist deep in these experts.

Few corporations hire priests. And the fact that very few corporations pay for religious counsel and advice may reveal a significant shift in allegiance. Modern corporate tribes buy scientific knowledge.

"Financial wizards" and "corporate headshrinkers" are staff men. Just as shamans and priests preside over rites-of-passage ceremonies, so also do psychologists lead assessment centers and conduct employment testing and interview sessions for new employees.

Witch doctors and soothsayers in the corporate tribe are scientists rather than holy men. They use scientific tools rather than revelations from God to look into the future.

The corporate tribes of the future, like their non-technological predecessors, will continue to avail themselves of advice from men-of-knowledge. Those which can attract and retain the best talent will have a powerful competitive advantage. The best talent will show their tribes how to apply the large quantities of fresh knowledge from science, especially those key bits of scientific knowledge which will contribute to the survival and growth of the tribe.

The god-kings are passing. The new chiefs are no longer divine. The men-of-knowledge have evolved into scientists who make no claims to "supernatural" powers. The worldwide population of tribal spirits, demons, ghosts and other supernatural beings has also been rapidly declining. The volcano gods, sea gods, wind gods are dying with the god-kings. Modern men-of-knowledge explain the world and their space-age miracles with science, and they have captured our attention. We have pinned our hopes on science, shifting much of our faith and allegiance from the traditional religions of the agricultural era.

Evolving Roles

Nature may be doing far more than percolating alphas to the tops of tribal pyramids. We may all be more or less drawn to our archetypal roles. Perhaps my own personality, abilities, interests and talents somehow led me to an ancient shaman career path. Perhaps those about me in corporate life, by responding to some behaviors and discouraging others, screened me out of some roles and led me into others. Perhaps we are all guided by half-buried understandings of tribal life that help us define our places in the tribe, our most effective ways to contribute.

Accountants, salesmen, engineers and advertising experts may not arrive in their specialized corporate roles by accident. They may be guided by dimly defined principles of selection, screening, and succession—a subconscious recognition of archetypal roles that have merely been refined by technology, rather than created new and fresh.

The new survival tasks have molded the roles of corporate tribesmen into altered forms—alpha has become a profit maximizer, the man-of-knowledge has become a scientist, the hunter a salesman, the gatherer a customer services representative, the slave a production worker. Recognizing our archetypal role may even help us to perform it better. The smooth and focused functioning of all the elemental tribal functions may yield faster growth and aid survival for modern corporations as they have done for earlier tribal adaptations.

Chapter Four

❧

ON STRENGTHENING CORPORATE TRIBES

IF we are tribal beasts, if human clusters organize and mobilize, consciously or unconsciously, their shared instincts for survival, then modern corporations which are unaware of their tribal roots may not be fully optimizing or focusing these innate group motivations.

Perhaps corporations are more like bee hives than we realize, having a sort of tribal mind that exists and grows, generation after generation, as an element of what Jung referred to as our "collective unconscious".

Clarifying our true nature should help to keep us squarely on evolution's trail. Perhaps we can even get our clumsy fingers on the fast switch and speed the process along. Perhaps, by more clearly recognizing elements of our tribal past which restrict us, we can more quickly emerge from its shell.

Most employees of modern corporations are more or less oblivious to the tribal nature of their organizations. Some top executives seem to harbor a dim recognition. The bulb glows when basic tribal concepts are presented.

This lack of awareness may inhibit corporations from achieving their full growth potential just as it may inhibit individuals within it. It is probable that corporate people clusters have many of the same traits of resilience, group inertia and survival drive that existed and worked in behalf of earlier tribes.

Commitment

Earlier men were occasionally called upon to fight and die for tribal preservation. Commitment was a real life and death issue. Commitment, esprit-de-corps, and selfless team effort were more quickly and easily mobilized in pre-industrial times, especially when the tribe was attacked. Adult males depended on one another for their lives. Each was aware of his own role and responsibilities, as well as his dependency on fellow tribesmen. History is replete with examples of men who died for their tribe. All cultures regard this selfless behavior as heroic.

The struggle for survival may still contribute to the climate of seriousness and no-nonsense which exists in many modern corporations. For millions of years, survival occasionally involved war. To survive, it was necessary to fight. The losers of a tribal war often lost more than control of their hunting territory. They also lost their wives and children. A loss frequently led to the systematic slaughter of adult males. These experiences were frequent enough so that survival had the most real and urgent of meanings. In this most serious business any show of levity in the ranks, any slight breakdown in discipline, would have resulted in a swift and forceful reprimand.

Modern corporations, by comparison, expect and get far more bland and passive commitments from their employees. They require no pledges of allegiance. No one is in imminent danger of being killed, maimed, or wounded.

Affiliations with churches, fraternal organizations, unions and political groups, as well as membership in the national tribe or the state may also serve to dilute an employee's corporate commitment. In modern industrial cultures, changing companies or being fired are common occurrences. Many college graduates fully expect to change companies several times in their careers. Executive search firms thrive on this operating tradition. Most tribes continue to grow even after major layoffs or leadership turnover. When a soldier is killed in battle, his survivors must quickly close ranks and press onward. Likewise, when an executive is fired or quits, few tears are shed. The survivors close ranks and press on.

These "limited commitment" values may be related to our love for the rebel, the entrepreneur, the outlaw and underdog. The theme of the noble individual, at war with the blind and immoral forces of the establishment, are common in Western culture. Many of our heroes are loners, individualists who do not conform to group pressures and expectations.

A great many employees, managers and executives are working for "number one." They work for money, for raises and promotions. If their personal goals are not met, and opportunities for advancement in another company present themselves, they go for it. This common form of self-interest on the part of the employee often has a flip side in shallow commitment of owners and officers to employees and subordinates. A slight alteration in strategy or corporate plans may result in the sacrifice of an operating unit, sale of a subsidiary or a cutback in employment. Decisions designed to maximize profits are sometimes made with little concern for a few hundred eliminated jobs. Sometimes eliminating jobs to cut payroll costs is the main objective.

The belief that the chief was God and that one's tribe was founded or chosen by God undoubtedly helped to strengthen commitment in earlier tribes. But these beliefs have not been widely applied to the corporate tribe. Nor have the religious ceremonies, shared secrets and rites-of-passage, so evident in earlier tribes, been given expression or form in the corporate tribe.

The results of all these elements are bland and shallow loyalties, distrust and manipulation. The employer uses the employee, withholding real loyalty and commitment. The employee uses the company as a stepping stone to further his or her own career, also withholding commitment.

Our growing understanding of the customs and traditions of Japanese corporations, with their cradle-to-grave commitments to employees, their frequent ceremonial pledges of allegiance, their company songs, shared vacations and concern for tribal elders; all these may be important ingredients in achieving high levels of productivity, quality products and services, and healthy growth.

In *Theory Z*[51], William Ouchi points out that early Japanese corporations may have had the advantage of absorbing agricultural tribes intact. Rather than attracting heterogeneous workers from the "rugged individualist" traditions of the frontier, Japanese industry absorbed entire farming villages. Corporate chiefs and elders merely replaced village chiefs and elders. Japan's rapid rise to industrial power may be the result of a better understanding of man's basic tribal nature, as well as operating traditions and policies which better focus and utilize man's basic, probably innate, desire for tribal affiliation.

Getting the Ax

Those at the top of corporate pyramids recognize the reality of their daily struggle for survival. They are constantly vigilant for those acquisition-minded predators who search for weak tribes. They fear each downturn in sales, each loss of market share, each rumor of a tender offer. They recognize that top leaders of corporations which are acquired often undergo a ritual sacrifice. As with tribes down through millions of years of evolution, the losers must do homage to the new rulers, escape to another tribe, or wait uncomfortably for the ax to fall.

The closest thing to being killed in modern corporations is being fired. Banishment, is infinitely more humane than being tortured, burned at the stake or decapitated. Like so many other evolved tribal activities, it is bloodless. But losing one's position of power, one's precarious perch in the pecking order, represents a real and ever-present danger for all modern executives.

Some executives are so absorbed in the struggle for tribal survival and growth that their families are neglected. For these tribesmen the hunt "is where it's at." They grind away at it, hating it and loving it, almost afraid to enjoy it.

Old-school executives are fearful of sharing profit information with employees. Some don't seem to regard employees as bona fide members of the tribe. They are seen as outsiders, as a necessary evil, paid slaves forever on trial, sometimes even as "the enemy." But without information, employees cannot identify with the objectives of the business. When they are ignorant of the profit picture, they are also unable to see how their work or the work of their department influences profits. Like a football team without an end zone, or a basketball team without a basket, the activities of these workers become aimless and spiritless.

Many behavioral scientists believe that organized labor feeds on these authoritarian attitudes of management. Unions have emerged and gained strength as a result of slavish management values and attitudes, and those organizations which consciously or subconsciously subscribe to the "divine rights" of management are fertile grounds for union organizers. When authoritarian pressures become unbearable and grievances cannot be aired without fear of retribution, workers will look to unions for redress. Everyone needs a tribe. Corporations which do not provide believable membership or ownership for workers may be unwittingly forcing workers into other tribes.

It is the coolness, the indifference, the fear, and the lack of fellowship and trust that many young people point to when they complain about careers in corporate organizations. Sometimes the change from college, with its many enthusiastic group events, to the activity of corporations is a bucket of cold water in the face. It is a change from parties, friends, dances, classes and an active social life to a serious, sober, intense and sometimes fear-laden climate.

By recognizing their own tribal identity, and by consciously modifying slave labor attitudes and beliefs that are a part of our agricultural heritage, corporations may be able to strengthen employee commitment and work in harmony with natural, perhaps hereditary, survival forces within their own organizations.

Corporations should actively strive to recapture and rebuild wholesome aspects of the tribal experience. To do it intelligently they should study other tribes, attempt to understand them, and identify those activities which could and should be emulated.

Corporation man is in the unique position of being able to see himself and his modern tribe in the new, much broader context of anthropological history. Those who use this knowledge to strengthen and improve their organizations will have a powerful survival advantage.

How to Strengthen Your Tribe

Executives who are interested in taking concrete steps to strengthen the tribal foundations of their organizations should seriously consider adapting some of the following program concepts:

Fire Fewer Employees

When owners and top executives of corporations see the tribe as their own, when they see workers as guests—as paid slaves, as a necessary evil, as production machines or appendages of machines, as a separate class, different from themselves—conditions for shallow commitment and alienation ripen.

Commitment is a two-way street. Loyalty is reciprocal.

The attitude on the part of management that it can easily get rid of employees has a mirror image in the attitude of workers. It is the attitude that if a worker does not like his job, he can easily change companies.

Where these attitudes of shallow commitment prevail in the minds of owners, management and workers, the corporation will fall short of its potential.

Shallow commitment in working relationships, as in marriages, is a form of denial of responsibility. Companies which lack a sufficient sense of responsibility to workers are quick to fire. They try to solve employee problems by getting rid of them. They feel little responsibility for training, coaching or helping workers improve their work. They abdicate responsibility for developing employees by relying on the "sink or swim" philosophy.

Employees who hear about or see fellow workers getting fired, dropping like trees in a storm, withhold full commitment from their corporations. They are like the sadder-but-wiser lover, cautious to surrender, fearful of another broken heart.

Full commitment requires a sense of belonging, a feeling of trust. For employees to willingly commit and work "like mad" for corporate growth, to defend their corporations and feel a sense of fulfillment within them, they need a reciprocal commitment from the corporation. They need job security, a feeling that they are valuable, needed and trusted by the corporation. They need assurance that the corporation will not abandon or sacrifice them in hard times.

Hundreds of corporate executives use threats of firing, as well as actual firing, as methods of pressuring and controlling employees. They believe withholding job security makes employees work hard. What they sow in fear they reap in shallow commitment.

Workers who see the corporation as a stepping stone in their own careers are also denying responsibility. They are withholding commitment and loyalty. Their contributions are for the ultimate objective of self-gain, rather than for tribal growth and survival. The fact that there are so many young, fast-track men and women who see their corporate employer as a two to three year training ground, with no intention of making a longer commitment, makes turnover inevitable. Some colleges, placement counselors and graduate schools actually encourage students to "shop around" before making a long-term commitment.

Corporate pyramids are, like all other dominance hierarchies, dynamic structures, constantly churning and reorganizing to accommodate new market conditions. This insures ongoing power struggles. The challenges of men who yearn to replace those above them in the corporate pecking order also assures turnover.

Firings and layoffs may also be the result of poorly controlled growth of manpower during good times. Given free reign, most department heads tend to add employees. Their desire to build internal empires may be part of the subtle forces which contribute to corporate growth.

Adding employees with too little planning or screening effort is another symptom of management indifference. The "easy come, easy go" approach to manpower planning and organization development gets many organizations into trouble. When profits are good, the temptation to hire is hard to resist. But the pain and expense of terminating employees when the payroll has become too huge to support, and the backlash of poor morale that sometimes lasts for years, have convinced many corporations to greatly strengthen their approach to forecasting and carefully controlling manpower growth.

The corporation that truly values its employees will be very careful about who joins the tribe. It will actively attempt to train and develop the talents of its employees, and tend to promote from within.

Japanese industry has demonstrated that cradle-to-grave commitment from management fosters loyalty in the attitudes of workers. These reciprocal commitments greatly ease labor relations, prevent strikes and result in high levels of worker cooperation and productivity. Relatively few Japanese workers rebel or complain about pay, policies, working conditions or the quality of their leadership. The average worker is a good citizen, self-effacing, obliging and willing to conform. He sees his corporation's growth as part of a national mission. To work hard is to be patriotic.

Corporate leaders, as well as workers in the U.S., need to rethink their ideas about allegiance and commitment. The concept of the corporation as a tribe will provide a common ground to help both workers and management meet their interdependent needs.

Achieve Profit Goals

Commitment may be influenced by the survival success of the tribe. Some unsuccessful tribes lack all semblance of commitment. Tribesmen spend their daily lives in a grim struggle for individual survival.

Colin Turnbull's[52] studies of the Ik in Central Africa show how stark, cold, and desperate a tribe can become. When an old woman falls from a rock ledge, weak from starvation, the tribesmen laugh at her. No one offers assistance. They too fight a daily battle to escape starvation. "Save the effort and the food for the living" is their motto.

The Tasady[53] represent an opposite point on the scale of humane cultures. Food is shared with meticulous fairness. Laughter, singing and open displays of affection are frequent occurrences.

In the workplace, commitment is influenced by the quality of relationships between workers, and by the degree to which workers feel they are participating in the success of the organization. These variables, in turn, influence the worker's sense of security within a corporation.

Mutual commitment varies considerably from one corporation to another, and from one department to another in the same corporation. In a committed work group, members know and like one another. They also respect one another's abilities and feel proud to be part of the group. In sports teams or fighting units of the armed forces, this attitude is referred to as "esprit de corps" or team spirit. It can contribute dramatically to a unit's motivation and success.

Organizations should actively work to develop this commitment. Where it exists things seem to go more smoothly. Group members still rise and fall in the pecking order, but the risings and fallings are not unduly disruptive. They can often be anticipated, so that promotions and changes in responsibility tend to confirm the group's own diagnosis, rather than surprise everyone.

Organizations with poor commitment are more vulnerable. The term "deadwood" is whispered about. Group members harbor fears about their own security. They cannot depend on rules. They often do not know other group members except on a superficial basis. They feel a constant, nagging sense of danger—not knowing what's going on.

*   *   *

I remember how individual commitment deteriorated in a large consulting operation during the recession of 1971. Because our clients were being cautious with their dollars, new consulting assignments were difficult to obtain. People became afraid of losing their jobs—with good reason. As the consulting staff ran out of work, staff reductions were made. The staff dwindled in size from 90 to 45 consultants over a nine-month period. Everyone looked at the Wall Street Journal advertisements for jobs, and lunch and coffee break discussions were grim and depressing.

Cooperation fell apart quickly. Rather than share the work, those who were able to obtain consulting assignments hoarded them, preserving their backlogs. It became "every man for himself". We knew we were losing money, and the psychology of failure had an erosive effect on morale.

There were many angry consultants, resentful of their lack of job security. There were frequent slashing criticisms of almost everything.

The cuts began at the bottom of the pecking order and worked upward. But it soon became clear that this approach tended to compound the problem. Since the top men with the heavier salaries remained, the average consulting fees per hour rose dramatically and the backlogs began to melt away even more quickly. When partners were not generating income, their heavy salary costs cut deeply into profits. Eventually the pressures of the recession eased and business improved. But the experience demonstrated how easily team spirit and commitment can be disrupted when the psychology of failure begins to take root.

★   ★   ★

Achieving difficult profit goals has the reverse effect. It stimulates feelings of pride in the tribe and by so doing, strengthens commitment.

Create More Ceremonies

In their book *Corporate Cultures*, Deal and Kennedy[54] identify some of the rites, rituals and ceremonies of corporate life. They make a convincing case for actively strengthening the cultural values of one's corporation. If one looks beneath the surface of everyday corporate activity, it is not difficult to recognize many of these rites and rituals.

But compared with more primitive tribes, the rites and rituals of corporations are indeed "beneath the surface." The rites and rituals of more primitive tribes represent the most colorful and expressive group activities that can be observed. They are anything but subtle and require no careful observation to detect.

It is important to note again that most of the major life events celebrated in earlier tribes are still celebrated. Marriages, funerals, naming ceremonies following new births—these still occur for modern men. But they do not occur in corporations. They happen in church. Even the important rites-of-passage that allows young people to join a corporation occurs at the high school or college auditorium rather than in the corporation.

But one ceremony is very common to corporations, and it tends to confirm that corporations are evolved hunting and warring entities. It is the war dance. At least once a year, sometimes more frequently, all the corporate hunters are called in from their territories. They plan campaigns, discuss the enemy, examine new sales tools and are introduced to new products or services. Many of the more successful sales meetings also get the troops fired up, motivated and inspired. Outside speakers skillful in delivering motivational messages are in great demand. Successful war dances, now as always, send the hunters back out into their territories with a new sense of confidence, invulnerability and courage.

Compared with many other tribes, modern corporations are often sober, serious, austere. Many primitive tribes had a rich variety of enjoyable group activities: feasts, celebrations and song-and-dance festivals that involved everyone in expressive, shared experiences. Church services, now and in agricultural times, provided similar tribal experiences.

Some large corporations are recognizing the importance of generating enthusiasm and hoopla in their corporate meetings. But many corporations still provide far too few meetings, discussions, classes, celebrations, ceremonies or employee activities. Some corporate leaders are suspicious of such activities, regarding them as a waste of time and money. The tribe needs arenas, places to assemble, to plan, to interact, to celebrate victories, places to sing and dance. The tribe needs a place "to happen".

For pre-technological tribes, ceremonies had immense importance. The first haircut, the first tooth, the first solid food, the first step, the first menses, the first kill, the first coitus, all were occasions for ceremonies. Ceremonies marked steps on each individual's career ladder in pre-technological tribes.

Among the Camaroons, birth of the first child enables the young wife to enter the group of full-fledged women. Elaborate initiation rites which mark the passage of boys into manhood are common in pre-technological tribes in all parts of the world. The Sioux Indians had no contact with Australian aborigines or the Kalihari of Africa, yet all practiced elaborate rites-of-passage ceremonies. The Jewish bar mitzvah, fraternity initiations, hazing in military schools, all offer modern-day parallels. Commencement in high schools and colleges is a modern rites-of-passage ceremony.

In most instances, the rites-of-passage ceremony secured for young initiates the right to participate as an adult in tribal ceremonies and activities. Often, such ceremonies involved vows from the initiate in exchange for the tribal sharing of mysteries, secrets or sacred objects. Some initiations were ordeals, including torturous measures, shaving the head, evulsion or filing of teeth, head-biting, immersion in dust or filth, heavy beating, scarification, tattooing, burning, circumcision and subincision.

Birth, marriage, death and burial, all locked in the traditions of each tribe, define for its members major life events. Ceremonies for planting, for harvest, for seasonal migration and hunts, provided tribes with a reoccuring calendar of events.

During a recent radio program, "The Native American Culture", a group of young Indians described the feelings they experienced during a powwow.

*   *   *

"It's really amazing to see how you can get just four or five guys together, you know, and one drum, and just some sticks, and you can make just hundreds of people move. You know, make hundreds of people happy and make hundreds of people all going at one time . . . in a circle, feeling all together . . . . And that all you have is that drum and those sticks and these guys' voices, you know.

Takes a lot out of the singers themselves . . . to sing them songs. But when you sing 'em good and you sing 'em the way people like 'em, you know—like a war dance—when we sing a war dance—we just put everything we got into it.

The Powwow or something—when it's going on—what you feel is, you feel really, everyone there is, you know, is really close to you. You really feel united. You feel like you're all one person, you know. You're just really having a good time. All your feelings are coming out, and . . . you're just sharing your feelings with everyone there."[55]

*   *   *

The cohesiveness of earlier tribes and the loyalty of individual members was strengthened by their almost continuous association with one another. They were together everyday. They could better identify and utilize each person's unique talents. Leadership evolved slowly, as young men matured and old men retired from the hunt. Survival was more clearly related to team effectiveness, as was the awareness of dependency on the group.

In America and Europe, most ceremonial activity still occurs in church. The familiar white steeple marks the central meeting place for tribal members. The ceremonies, the group singing, the common religious belief, the priests in his black robes, all of these provide the arena and the traditions essential for a rich and rewarding tribal life. Our fathers and grandfathers were largely farmers who belonged to agricultural tribes. The chief was the priest, pastor, or bishop—a spokesman for God.

For many men and women, the church service still provides an intensely supportive tribal experience. Almost everything is predictable. One knows when to rise, when to sit and what phrases of speech are appropriate in prayers. And when the members rise together and sing the words of a familiar song, the sensation of group unity and solidarity is unmistakable. For most people, the feeling is intensely satisfying. This feeling of group unity has been known for millions of years.

Ceremony is glue for tribes. It provides shared experience. As such, it is a key element in establishing traditions, loyalty, identification, commitment and a sense of corporate culture.

Some earlier tribal ceremonies provided psychological rewards that may be difficult for modern corporations to match. Consider the celebration following a successful hunt.

★   ★   ★

The men are laughing and reliving their adventure. The women and children are listening. A hunter performs a ceremonial dance for his fascinated audience. He demonstrates how carefully he stalks his prey, how he takes aim, how he drives his spear home. His companions, his relatives, his children, his group, beam with pride and share happily in the meat of the celebration feast. In such a setting, the rewards in terms of tribal approval are rich, strong and, from a psychological viewpoint, nourishing. They are results-oriented. They are ego-building. The hunter feels a deep sense of acceptance, of contribution, of belonging. For a time, he is a tribal hero.

*   *   *

Ceremony builds commitment. It creates cohesiveness. Occasions for group meetings, celebrations for a successful hunt, a rich harvest, marriages, initiation rites, shared secrets, shared ordeals, religious worship—all of these experiences bind participants together by providing group identification. The liturgy and repetition of ceremonies is essential for allowing maximum audience participation. If a participant "knows the words", he is accepted by the others and responds with a feeling of identification with the group.

Because corporations are evolved hunting groups, and because churches still preside over most of the important life ceremonies, corporations have relatively few regularly occurring events that might contribute to a feeling of belonging, unity, or esprit de corps.

*   *   *

At 10:30 I was given a slip of paper with a typewritten line on it. It was my part in the annual stockholders meeting.

The leadership was assembled in front—all the chiefs, looking very chiefly. Several of them gave brief reports on the activities of their sub-tribes. The stockholders filled a large auditorium. Everyone was curious about everyone else. Many fellow employees greeted one another, smiles on faces.

I found myself an actor in a tribal ceremony.

At 11:20, the corporate director of personnel tossed me my cue. I arose and called out my lines, loud and clear.

I cued another employee stockholder who "seconded" my motion.

The meeting followed the script well. Like myself, all the actors from the floor and the podium dutifully spoke their lines.

Several corporate leaders had been ill-at-ease regarding the meeting. Their major fear was some minority stockholder asking embarrassing questions. Fortunately, Ralph Nader did not show up.

At noon the meeting was over—no serious questions or disruptions from the floor—all the business taken care of—largely because profits were high and the shareholders were feeling good.

★   ★   ★

But that annual stockholders meeting fell far short of its potential. Following a good year, it should have been a celebration. Reward good performance!

Corporations need more success celebrations. They can be a powerful form of reward that encourages continued excellence.

Most corporations have evolved a loosely woven fabric of ceremonial events. The common ones include the annual stockholders meeting, board meetings, planning sessions, sales meetings, service award ceremonies, retirement dinners, Christmas parties and, sometimes, an annual dinner-dance. Recently some management groups have introduced meetings among workers to discuss working conditions, quality problems and production procedures. Quality Circles, currently in use with many forward-thinking manufacturers, provide such opportunities. They enhance worker participation, motivation and productivity.

Many regularly scheduled meetings eventually develop a sort of ceremony. But most of these ceremonial occasions in corporations could, and should, be consciously strengthened. Effective meetings can reward outstanding performance, establish corporate traditions, recognize heroes and build a clearer sense of corporate mission.

Clarify Tribal Roles

Will all the tribal elders please rise. Thank you elders.

Now could we have the chiefs and sub-chiefs. All rise, please. Thank you chiefs.

Will all the hunters please rise. Thank you hunters.

Now can we have the shamen, please. First the wise men and sorcerers. Now the apprentices, please. Good.

Now we are going to ask all the gatherers to rise. All rise please. Thank you ladies.

Now the slaves, please. Thank you.

With a brief introductory lecture, in some gigantic hall filled with a multitudinous congregation of corporate employees, most would have little difficulty recognizing their archetypal roles.

Knowing one's role in a corporation helps one to perform it better.

*   *   *

I was meeting with a client one day when one of their top men called me into his office, closed the door behind us, and thanked me for something I had said in a seminar two years earlier. I was a bit embarrassed but also deeply pleased.

I had helped the man more clearly recognize his role, his responsibility, and his power as a tribal elder.

In his early sixties, he was a man who, by word and deed, exuded a rare aura of wholesomeness and integrity. He was also a very humble man who clearly underestimated his power. He was trusted by everyone.

He was nearing retirement age, did not want to retire, and was fearful that his organization was thinking about replacing him. For this reason, he was holding back, not really pressing his views in top-level corporate policy meetings.

I had reminded him that one source of power for an elder was that their opinions were often regarded as in the best interest of the tribe as a whole. Once an executive is past the stage of active competition for the alpha position, others tend to be less suspicious of his underlying motives and hidden agendas. The views of elders are often regarded as less self-serving and, therefore, more persuasive than the views of younger and more ambitious men. Elders also carry the powerful trappings of wisdom and seasoned experience.

I had also reminded him of his role as a historian and a transmitter of tribal traditions. I had encouraged him to speak out in policy meetings, to share his early memories and stories of the tribe with younger employees, to accept his role as a mentor and to remind others, especially alpha and top line executives, of the failures and successes of the past.

Our discussion had helped him to clarify his role. He enjoyed thinking of himself as an elder.

★   ★   ★

Women executives who have attended my lectures are sometimes disturbed by the references to male bonding, male leadership and male dominance hierarchies. They are concerned when they realize that male resistance to their ascendancy in the corporate pecking order may be the result of millions of years of evolution.

It is important for women executives to understand the tribal nature of corporations. If corporations are evolved hunting and warrior activities, and if women and children were excluded from these activities in earlier tribal adaptations, it follows that women executives may have a lot of subconscious attitudes to overcome.

★   ★   ★

I met with a woman executive who had called me to see if I could help her find a new position. After several years as a department head, she had been fired. She was very capable and intelligent. Like anyone who gets banished from a tribe, she was also angry and deeply resentful of the man who had fired her.

As she told the story of her deteriorating relationship with her boss, I realized that she did not understand the tribal nature of her organization.

She had a tendency to see her employees as children. She had a substantial amount of nurturance in her temperament, and no children of her own to soak it up, so the tendency to view herself in a mothering role was probably natural.

She also tended to see the president in a father role. Her concept of the company was clearly drawn from the family model.

She relied on this model extensively—mother, father, and children—and it influenced the way she handled her administrative responsibilities.

She conducted long counseling sessions with her employees and seemed fulfilled when they were willing to share intimate details of their daily lives. When the president put pressure on the "family", she saw her role as one of cushioning them from the pressure. She tried to develop and preserve feelings of closeness and belonging among her employees.

Her greatest mistake was probably her tendency to challenge the profit motive. To her, good morale was far more important than reaching difficult sales and production targets.

I encouraged her to abandon the family model in thinking about corporate work groups. There are no children in corporate tribes. I encouraged her to think of work groups as hunters or warriors involved in a very serious, no-nonsense game of survival. I encouraged her to develop her own hunting skills—buy a shotgun and learn how to use it.

She looked at me as though I did not have both oars in the water. She completely ignored my advice.

*   *   *

Hunters and warriors carry weapons. For millions of years, they killed to survive. Women who seek line management responsibilities and want to compete with men must become tough, assertive, competitive, even predatory. Unless some male competitor is calling her a "bitch", she is probably not being assertive enough.

The skills required to be a production manager, to direct a group of workers, are similar to the skills required to lead a squad in battle. One must give orders, coordinate efforts, check on progress and assure that the objective is achieved. Too much tender loving care may make hunters soft and vulnerable.

If you want to be a shaman, you must master some area of needed knowledge or information, something the tribe must know to survive. Become a tax specialist, a financial wizard, a computer whiz, a high-powered attorney a futurist or head-shrinker. If you want to be a super shaman, strive to become a consultant. Get an advanced degree. Become an authority. Write a book.

I have a cousin, younger than I, an escaped sorcerer's apprentice. After several years of advanced physics, trying to count neutrinos, he switched majors. With a degree in operations research from Wharton, he joined the marketing department of an airline. Now he analyzes traffic flow, the thousands of passengers that board aircraft day after day. He then recommends changes in flight frequencies and schedules to maximize the number of passengers per airplane for his tribe. He works it out with math and computer models.

In this sense, he is a scout. He rides on ahead of the tribe and brings back information. The leaders use it to locate the herds and investigate the enemy. The information helps them to decide which course to take, where to set up camp.

Recognizing that clerical workers are evolved gatherers and that production workers are evolved slaves can help to strengthen corporations. The knowledge will help eliminate more physically exhausting and mentally unchallenging jobs. By recognizing the slave archetype in our values and attitudes toward blue collar, hourly, non-exempt employees, we can consciously work toward improvement in employee relations. This can be accomplished by sharing plans and operating information with workers, by encouraging employee stock purchases, by more frequent recognition of contributions, by programs to actively assist in developing needed skills and craftmanship, and by meetings designed to strengthen tribal commitment and pride.

Remove Barriers To Corporate Unity

The corporate tribesman has a difficult time forming a sense of loyalty and belonging to his group because the architecture of modern office buildings keeps him holed away in his own cubicle, and the scattered nature of operating units make large tribal meetings impractical. Some modern tribesmen rarely see their leaders in action. They observe very few tribal traditions and rarely join with others in ceremonies, celebrations or large-scale tribal events. They occasionally see fellow tribesmen and women quitting or getting fired. They see new tribesmen and women entering the corporation from outside. They often live under a cloud of suspicion, criticism or fear.

Corporate office buildings which separate various office areas and divide the tribe into floors may inhibit employees from forming a sense of identity and loyalty.

*   *   *

Mary Jane works in the audit section on the 21st floor. Every day, she catches the 7:20 bus, gets off at the corner of Fifth and Walnut, walks two blocks to the office building, rides the elevator to 21, gets off, turns right at the lobby and right again down the hallway to the audit section. Her desk is the third one back in the second row. Over the years, she gets acquainted with the other employees in the audit section. The Controller, an important subchief, is her only contact with management. The last time she saw the president was four months ago when he happened to get on the elevator she was riding.

She sees other employees in the coffee room but never really gets to know them. Her concept of the corporation is limited by the walls and personalities of the audit section.

There are thousands like her. They work in the engineering area, the personnel section, the sales area. Most have highly restricted concepts of their tribe.

*   *   *

Earlier tribes often arranged huts around a central open area which provided a convenient place for ceremonies. The dances, feasts, visits from outsiders, arrivals and departures; all occurred in view of all the tribespeople. Each tribal member could participate in tribal activities. They could keep track of the comings and goings of the chief. Unlike corporate employees who are sealed off from visual contact, pre-technological tribespeople organized themselves in a way that contributed to active participation in tribal events.

Corporations seeking unity should actively compete with outside groups to capture discretionary time and become a part of the social lives of their employees. Corporations should encourage the development of friendships at work, sponsor social events, sports teams, glee clubs, hobby groups and meetings where employees can get acquainted with their leaders.

During normal working hours, corporations must work toward survival and growth. They must hunt for sales and produce quality goods and services. But after hours, they should organize get-acquainted parties, training programs, choruses, bands, exercise classes, bowling and softball teams, folk dancing groups and continuing education programs.

Corporations should organize tours to subsidiary and division operating units to help employees visualize and understand the size and scope of their corporate tribe.

Increase Leadership Visibility

Tribes of people, like other primate clusters, focus on alpha. The chief is and always has been a focal point, a magnet for the attention of his tribespeople. At intervals, they steal a look at the leader. They both love and fear him. They may derive a sense of security from him. As stated earlier, in hunting-gathering and agricultural tribes the chief was god-like, divine, or divinely inspired. Smart corporations will work to ensure that this perceived leader power works for, not against them.

Corporations should work on making their leadership more visible. In many corporations, employees seldom see their leaders in action. Our vertical corporate villages seal the leaders

off from employees, in their own separate cubicles. Geography
and our compartmentalized architecture work against visible
leadership.

*   *   *

I was sitting on a beautiful white beach in Florida, the
sun feeling delicious, my wife beside me.

In front of us in the surf were six of the top executives
of an $800 million food conglomerate. I was helping to run
an executive retreat—lectures and discussions in the morn-
ings and evenings, tennis and golf in the afternoons, gourmet
meals. It was outstanding.

My attention focused on alpha. He was there in the frothy
water, holding his wife's arm, gently leading her into the
surf. Both had big grins on their faces, like children, as the
first wave washed across her swimsuit.

In that instant I learned something new about the president. I had seen him in a new way—out of his office, out
of his suit and tie—in a tender moment.

*   *   *

This corporation held three top management sessions each
year, with spouses. They were regarded as an important form
of non-cash compensation. They also provided a vehicle for
stimulating the thinking and awareness of company leaders.
The president always took an active part, and his leadership
helped strengthen the executive core group. Over several years,
the corporation had little turnover. Its executive group achieved
challenging objectives year after year, and these sessions were
one of the reasons. They strengthened the organization by pro-
moting shared experiences, friendships and team effort among
the executives and their spouses, and by providing a tribal arena
where alpha and other leaders could interact.

One method for increasing the visibility of alpha and other
leaders in corporations is closed circuit television. Large screens
can be set up in conference rooms and work areas where many
employees can assemble. Monthly briefing sessions from cor-

porate headquarters, or from the heads of the respective sub-tribes or operating units, are an effective method for passing along operating information, unveiling plans and clarifying objectives.

The systems should include hookups to allow television meetings, discussions and picture transmissions between major operating units. If MacNeil and Lehrer can do it, corporations can do it. They really should get on with it. The technology is here. We could use the energy saved in less travel.

Encourage Respect for Tribal Elders

Recognizing that corporations are tribes helps to more clearly identify the elders. They are sprinkled throughout large organizations; the career professionals, the most experienced, long-service employees, mostly out of contention for alpha, resigned to the reality that they will retire from somewhere beneath the top of the dominance hierarchy.

These veterans are the transmitters of tribal knowledge. They hold the history of the corporation, the liturgy of past chiefs in their memories. They remember the inside stories and experiences of the tribe. They know the life histories of the owners and their families, the internal politics and the collection of personalities at the top of the pyramid.

Many of these veterans feel used and unappreciated as they near retirement. They are often referred to as "out to pasture", and the phrase is turgid with archetypal meaning. They are often less actively involved with the hunting and warring of the tribe. They are advisors, past their prime breeding and child-rearing years. They are grandparents, mellow, relaxed, seasoned.

Many corporations do honor them. Photographs of 30-year veterans appear in the company newspaper. Award ceremonies, service awards, retirement dinners—all are designed to honor elders. Some organizations do a good job of it. Others do not. They undervalue the advice of their elders and seldom seek it.

The brightest leaders know how to seek and benefit from the counsel and advice of tribal elders. Men who are too young or too independent to seek the advice of elders make more frequent errors.

Create Corporate Totems

In some primitive tribes, men and women believed they literally descended from animals. Within a tribe, there were typically several clan groups, each identified by a different totem animal. If their totem animal was a jaguar, as in some South American tribes, or an emu, as in some Australian tribes, the people of that clan group treated their totem animal with special reverence and respect. They performed dances to honor their totem animal, and believed they personally possessed that animal's admirable and peculiar traits.

Membership in a given clan group had a major impact on one's life. For example, it was normally taboo to marry someone in one's own clan group. Even primitive men recognized the taboo against "dipping one's pen in company ink". Traces of these ancient beliefs have been handed down and can be found in such symbols as the Russian bear, the lion of England and the American golden eagle.

When I had occasion to do some consulting with Flying Tiger Line, a multinational air freight corporation, I found that the tiger symbol has a powerful influence on the employees of the corporation. Paintings, prints, calendars, photographs and ceramic sculptures of tigers are proudly displayed in offices from top executives down to cubby-hole work areas of the secretarial typing pool. The logo of the Tiger face appears on the corporate stationery. It is painted on the sides and doors of delivery trucks. It plays a prominent part in national advertising campaigns. Employees refer to two corporate office buildings as "High Tiger" and "Low Tiger". Veteran employees are called "old Tigers".

More than one executive has told me: "I've always been a Tiger. I'm from L.S.U.;" or, "My high school team was the

Tigers." Some seem to feel that being a Tiger was somehow part of their destiny.

The Tiger symbol clearly has less compelling spiritual meaning to employees of Flying Tiger than it had as a totem of more primitive men. After all, Darwin has convinced most scientists that we really descended from ape-like creatures. Even though no employees of Flying Tiger believe they descended from tigers, the symbol acts as an amazingly powerful and emotionally charged force.

Corporations which use stylized letters, or family names for their symbol also appear able to create employee and customer loyalty. Certainly, IBM, GE, and ITT have achieved worldwide recognition. Madison Avenue has earned millions in creating simple, catchy, modern-looking corporate logos.

But few of those who create corporate logos recognize or use the archetypal history of the symbols they choose. Both Freud and Jung frequently referred to the fact that archaic symbols surface in dream images and art forms of modern as well as primitive men and women.

I believe that Flying Tiger's corporate name and symbol get much more "bang for the buck" than those of the average corporation. Their totem animal, I believe, contributes to employee loyalty and commitment. Since the airline operates in the Orient, it may also arouse ancient subconscious associations that are deeply imbedded in Oriental cultures.

In *Corporate Cultures*,[56] Deal and Kennedy point out the importance of slogans or mottos that reflect basic corporate values. DuPont's "better things for better living through chemistry", or Hallmark's "when you care enough to send the very best" are examples. These slogans reflect basic values and beliefs that contribute to building a corporation's basic culture. They focus employee values and create themes by which customers and suppliers define the corporation. They may have a far more powerful impact than most organizations realize and should be carefully researched and consciously applied to contribute to survival and growth.

Give Employees A Piece of the Action

Employee Stock Ownership Programs (ESOP), probably provide the single most direct method for a corporation to purposely work toward strengthening commitment of tribespeople.

An ESOP is an employee benefit plan designed to invest in the securities of the employer. It provides a financially attractive method for corporations to help employees become stockholders.

Employee Stock Ownership Programs get to the root of the problem of employee commitment. Corporate blue collar workers are the evolved slave labor of agricultural man. In the era of agriculture, tribespeople who were conquered were either slain or carried off into captivity. They became slaves, people without territory. Early corporate leaders were nearer to the cutting edge of the transition from agriculture. To them, the employees were still more like slaves than fellow tribesmen.

The main advantage of ESOP programs is that they acknowledge the employee as a full-fledged member of the tribe, an owner of shares. This clearly strengthens employee commitment and loyalty. It also helps destroy the slave-labor attitudes held by our agricultural predecessors.

Shallow commitment to workers is usually reciprocated. The more management exploits its workers, the more workers despise management. The more management defines workers as separate from themselves, the more workers are inclined to join forces against management.

We all need tribal affiliations. Unions are the result of management groups which have excluded workers from membership in the tribe. ESOPs help to correct this remnant of slavery values in corporate philosophy. They also help quell the not-so-subtle civil war that often rages between management and unions in many modern corporations.

Ideally, *each new employee should be given one share of company stock on the day he or she is hired*. It should be part of the welcoming and orientation ceremony for new employees.

This ceremony should replace prevalent probationary and trial periods for new employees, which currently start thousands of workers under a cloud of fear, doubt and suspicion. Probationary policies usually suggest to the new employee that he can be fired quickly if he is found unacceptable for any reason in the first few months. It is step one in a fear conditioning process within many current corporations.

Employees should gain increasing shares of stock as they rise in the corporate pecking order. Employees should be awarded stock at five, ten, fifteen, twenty, twenty-five, and thirty-year award ceremonies.

Companies should use dollars currently being awarded as cash bonuses to managers to buy their own stock. This, rather than cash, should be awarded on the basis of measured performance against clearly defined objectives.

As with all other forms of corporate compensation, the award and accumulation of shares should reflect an employee's position in the pecking order.

Distribution of stock awards, especially in the form of stock options, is a well-established practice within modern corporations, but only top executives normally benefit from this form of capital sharing.

ESOPs provide a vehicle to expand such programs so that all employees may benefit. Giving shares, spreading the ownership, frees the slaves. Then, every day, both the chairman and the newest secretary can look at the stock listings in the newspaper. The entire tribe's attention can be frequently focused on the same important number—the price of the stock. Everyone should want it to grow. A mystic might think that all those positive vibrations, all those focused thoughts, all that tribal energy working together, might create a powerful force—perhaps a self-fulfilling prophesy.

A Tribe Builder

Since my early stages of research on tribal roles, I have realized that I am an evolved shaman—a headshrinker. I know that I cannot claim divine inspiration, as did my predecessors in agricultural or hunting-gathering tribes. My knowledge must come from science. My success as a corporate shaman depends on how effective I am in strengthening the survival potential and growth performance of my client tribes.

I make no apologies for subscribing to the motives of profit and growth. I have deep reservations about those who are encouraging no growth, or zero growth, as a basic planning concept. Growth has always been an essential objective for tribes. There will always be tribes which aggressively fight and struggle for it with all their resources. Those tribes which consciously abandon growth as an essential objective are simply leaving the battlefield of survival to those who are less timid.

Recognizing that modern corporations, like all the tribes which preceded them, are struggling for growth and survival helps to justify the validity of the profit motive. It also helps employees clarify their roles within the tribe.

Each employee, at every level, in every department, should ask, "What can I do best to contribute to the health, the growth, and the survival of my tribe?"

In my own case, the answer was clear when I was finally able to ask the question in this way. I could help my client tribes build and strengthen the quality of their leadership.

I tried to conceptualize it as a quality-control problem. I realized that if I could influence the through-put—the stream of managers that was percolating into leadership positions—I could gradually upgrade the quality of management.

I could also screen individuals hired from outside the organization and help to assure that this input was, in fact, strengthening rather than diluting the quality of the existing management group.

In addition, I could help managers to recognize their archetypal roles, strengthen their commitments to the tribe, and identify and fully develop their best talents.

Many management psychologists like myself are providing services and programs for corporations that are designed to strengthen the quality of management. One fast-growing method is the Development Center. Some programs are called Assessment Centers, and they are a bit ruthless. Employees are required to attend, and those who do poorly can say goodbye to their future career plans in the company. Some of these assessment centers create fear and, inadvertently, undermine commitment, team effort and morale.

The newly emerging management retreats among some Japanese corporations are like Assessment Centers but far more strenuous. In fact they bear all the ear markings of a tribal rites-of-passage. At a certain stage in their careers, Japanese managers are sent to an extended "training session" in the mountains. Participants are dressed in strange costumes, forced to memorize company policies, sing company songs, endure physical exercise and stand for long periods at attention. The pressure is so intense that many managers are reduced to tears before finally being "passed".

I strongly support this rebirth of rites-of-passage ceremonies within corporations, but I feel it is not essential to "knock out teeth".

Rather than threaten employees with possible firing or limited future growth, these programs should be designed to strengthen commitment and build self-esteem. Every employee should be encouraged to buy stock and to remain with the company until retirement. This orientation is important, if one is seeing the company as a tribe.

When the purpose is limited to assessment, the implication is that some will be screened out. Granted, this may be a rapid way to upgrade the quality of management. But it can leave deep wounds and aftershocks of fear and distrust that can be a serious drawback to a tribe's ability to survive.

To survive, the tribe must work together smoothly. It is important that the tribespeople trust each other and have confidence in each other's ability. Those who talk about "deadwood" in the corporation, or divide their management into "acceptable" and "unacceptable" employees, are expressing poor levels of faith in the tribe as a whole. They are undermining morale and commitment.

Threatening employees with possible firing is classical Theory X. Even the term Assessment Center has a certain Hitlerian ring. Ach-tung! The clicking of heels.

In a Development Center, a small group of executives goes through a week-long series of realistic management exercises. Each exercise is followed by peer feedback. At the conclusion, reports are prepared giving specific advice to help each participant identify and more fully develop his or her commitment and team orientation as well as administrative and leadership skills. Recommendations are also prepared to identify and strengthen areas of potentially weak performance. These recommendations may include attendance at university or trade association courses for executives, classes in public speaking, assertiveness training or speed reading. They can include job rotation programs or assignment to special task force projects. They may also include programs to improve health and fitness, such as weight-loss clinics and exercise programs.

The corporation's management development specialist schedules the seminars and helps with the follow-up to assure that the grooming programs are actually accomplished. Periodic review sessions are also conducted so that managers can be guided into positions that make full use of their talents and minimize the impact of their weaknesses.

Properly designed and conducted, Development Centers are an effective tool for building and strengthening the quality of management. By gradually upgrading management, they contribute directly to tribal survival and growth.

They are also an ancient kind of tribal retreat where selected managers leave the compound to go into the woods with a shaman and experience a type of ritual sharing of tribal secrets.

Testing outside candidates to assure client tribes do not inadvertently dilute the quality of their management group, and helping to identify high-potential managers and improve their leadership and administrative skills, can gradually strengthen the quality of an organization's management.

Wizard Power

We wizards do have certain powers. I once turned an executive into a goat. He had become so caught up in an unbridled pursuit of hedonistic pleasures that the women in the typing pool were no longer safe. His appetite for drugs, booze and sex, and his unrelenting search for entertainment were steadily eroding his effectiveness. Like a goat, he was always horny. He would eat anything.

I told him he was becoming an old goat. I pointed out how hairy he was becoming and asked if his feet and forehead were sore from the formation of hooves and horns. I told him how others had noticed his smelly breath when he returned from lunch. He was becoming a bit disgusting. His job was in danger.

Of course, his goatness was self-induced. I merely held up a mirror so he could see himself more clearly.

By far my best feat of wizardly magic is turning corporations into tribes. It is also done with mirrors. This book is a mirror. Lecturing on corporate tribe concepts seems to remove the scales from the eyes of employees. Many see their corporations in a new way. The corporation, as a tribe, can be useful if regarded only as a metaphor. Of course, I see it as much more than a metaphor. Because I see my clients as tribes, and can speak directly to their tribal souls, I can create a powerful new awareness. I believe the knowledge contributes to employee morale, strengthens commitment and improves productivity. It's a wonderful trick. I enjoy performing it.

Current Evolutionary Trends

As each new theory is put forth, Theory X, MBO, quality circles, Theory Z; something rubs off. Things rarely change as rapidly as the theorists want. There seems to be an ample supply of experts eager to present new criticism and theories of corporate activity. But as each new wave of knowledge washes over the thousands of corporate managers, some improvements do occur.

There are many indications of steadily improving working conditions within modern corporations. Much of it has resulted directly from a more generous sharing of information and responsibility with workers. It took almost two decades of unremitting yammering from behavioral scientists to modify authoritarian Theory X attitudes in corporations, but the effort is clearly paying off. More employees are getting involved in planning, in participative and results-oriented approaches to management. More corporations are informing employees of key operating information, including plans, profits and details of their compensation programs and benefits. More employees than ever own stock in their companies. Management-by-objectives concepts are penetrating into schools, governments, and deeply into the many operating units of highly diversified corporations. Work is more satisfying when employees work with clearly defined objectives.

Computerized management information systems are providing increasingly fast and accurate measures of performance. The need for stern and strong supervisors to "check on" the workers is disappearing.

Many corporations are restructuring jobs, making them more intellectually challenging, weeding out those which are boring and repetitive. It's called job enrichment. It works.

In Search of Excellence[57] is a recent book that promises to have a powerful influence on corporate thinking and practice. Its practical, common-sense approach provides excellent advice on how to practice fundamental principles of good management. Its authors, Peters and Waterman, speak in the language of the corporate tribe.

Yet, these experienced McKinsey consultants seem only to nibble around the edges of tribology. They espouse clear metaphors, and encourage the development of symbols, rituals, and myths, but the metaphor of a corporation as a tribe, is still poorly developed.

The term "Corporation Tribes" appeared in Anthony Jay's book, *Corporate Man*.[58] A chapter entitled "Corporate Tribes" was also included in the book *Corporate Cultures* by Deal and Kennedy[59]. These authors have made valuable contributions.

Authors of both *Corporate Cultures* and *In Search of Excellence* encourage leaders to develop a stronger "culture" within their corporations. Anthropologists would probably object to using the term "culture" to describe a specific company's motto or operating philosophy. They may, in fact, point out that all American corporations are part of the same culture. All have the same basic values and operating traditions. All speak the same language. All wear similar costumes, use similar building designs, eat similar foods and see the same television programs.

In fact, these well-meaning authors may have created as much confusion as clarification in using the term "culture" so loosely. Yet the term was used in a good cause. Perhaps excellent companies do have a more clearly defined emphasis on quality, or people, or customer services.

On the other hand, I have encountered *no* corporations which would *not* subscribe to these common values. It would be a form of blasphemy for any corporation to argue against the importance of quality products, good customer relations or the importance of people. These *are* motherhood concepts, and the fact that the authors anticipated the criticism doesn't really help.

Perhaps excellent companies *are* those which are most successful in really applying these basic motherhood concepts, rather than merely giving them lip service.

Rather than search for excellence and create stronger cultures, whatever that term may mean, corporate managers should go straight to the heart of the matter. They should create a tribe. The tribal analogy is clean and clear and easy for even the newest employee to understand. And the task of becoming a tribe is easy, like swimming downstream, because all corporations are tribes already, so the task becomes a simple process of peeling back the top layers of the onion, telling employees who they really are, helping them clarify their roles and accept the basic survival mission of their tribe.

In Search of Excellence discourages management groups from using the military as a metaphor to describe their activities.[60] They seem to encourage the use of the "family" metaphor. In this respect, the book misses a fundamental principle of corporate evolution: Families have children, but corporations are comprised only of adults.

Corporations evolved from armies. As discussed earlier, the farmer soldier and the hunter-warrior are anthropological antecedants to the modern day worker. All nation-states still employ full-time soldiers. They still attempt to secure nation-state boundaries with standing armies. And all are prepared to increase the size of their armies by requiring military services from corporate employees. In times of emergency, the blue-collar workers become foot soldiers. The college-educated managers become officers. Thus, the same class stratification that exists in all tribes, in all cultures, merges smoothly into fighting units when threats to the territory of the nation-state occur.

The reason that military compaigns offer such compelling analogies to corporate managers, and are so frequently used to describe corporate campaigns, is that they *are* very similar— the most recent preceding link is evolution's chain.

Seeing one's operating unit as a family is dangerously nurturant. Too much tender-loving-care may sap the fighting power of an operating unit. Treating employees as children and seeing the president as daddy are seriously off-target.

Corporations are not, and should not be regarded as families. They are evolved food-getting entities. The hunter/gatherer roles are beginning to break down in terms of male/female segregations. However, they are still *primarily* segregated. The men are primarily hunters. They must be ruthless and uncompromising in searching for and closing contracts and sales. Now as always, they must protect, defend and expand tribal territory.

Women are still primarily gatherers. They too are actively involved in feeding the tribe. Every customer contact should be treated as a tender plant, nurtured, fed, protected and carefully harvested. Gatherers also play a major role in feeding the tribe.

It is important to recognize that every adult, male or female, shares in the responsibility for "feeding" the tribe. All must be constantly aware that care and feeding of the customer herd, the customer crop, is critical to a good harvest.

It is also important to recognize that every tribe with a similar product line wants to take over your cropland and steal your herd. They also need food. They also have people to feed.

The thousands of youthful critics of corporations apparently do not realize that joining some kind of tribe is almost inescapable. Even if a young person avoids corporate life, he or she is likely to join a government organization, a school district, a not-for-profit organization. All are tribes. All include the dreaded dominance hierarchy, the authority figures, and the no-nonsense struggle for survival.

A few people start their own tribes. But the vast majority become tribesmen and tribeswomen, competitors for dominance, members of some pyramid-shaped human cluster. It is best to face up to this reality, choose your tribe carefully, join it, mentally pledge your allegiance, try to acquire shares, and work with diligence for its survival and growth.

Chapter Five

❧

ON THE
EVOLUTION
OF
CORPORATE TRIBES

A few short years ago, some scattered stone tools and bits of jawbone represented the only scraps of evidence available to explain man's evolution. Today, at hundreds of digs throughout the world, archeologists are unearthing layer after layer of pre-history. Their analysis, dating, and cataloging of artifacts, stone tools, and animal and human bones is yielding an intriguing picture of man's emergence.

The oldest recognizable bits of humanoid jawbone unearthed, as of this writing, are 14,000,000 years old. They belonged to a strange apelike creature which is now gone. So are most of the various strains and types of our humanoid predecessors which formed other links in the evolution of man.

Fossil remains of more recent human-like creatures over one million years old have now been found in Europe, Africa, East Asia, Java, and China. These fossil remains represent races of manlike creatures which are also gone. There may be dozens of varieties of men which are now either extinct, or have evolved into new forms.

An anthropologist by the name of Ralph Holloway,[61] has been pouring plaster into some of these ancient skulls. The skulls, serving as molds, allow scientists to create plaster castings of ancient human brains. Such castings, made from skulls of modern as well as ancient men, allow researchers to create tables and trend lines of the human brain's evolutionary history.

The brain—a humming, blood-rich, electrochemical computer, made up of densely packed nerve cells—for how many million years was this evolving computer merely a glowing ember, a dim light? This tool for survival, this gradually emerging intelligence, how accurately did it light the world?

Holloway points out that the shape of the brain provides a more accurate key to identifying human qualities than the shape of the skull. His plaster casts suggest that man's brain began to differ from other primates about three million years ago. By calculating the ratio between brain volume and body weight (in modern man this is 1:45), trend lines can be traced back into pre-history.

Modern man has an average weight of 150 pounds and a cranial capacity of 1,361 cubic centimeters. Evidence suggests that our earlier relatives, from one to three million years ago, were much smaller. Some authorities estimate the body weight of Australopithecine to be between 50 and 75 pounds! He stood about 4 feet tall. His brain, though essentially human, with the same enlarged frontal lobe as modern man, was smaller. Although he could probably reason and make use of abstract symbols, he was probably far less intelligent than modern man.

Holloway's plaster casts of three million year old brains have essentially the same structure and configuration as modern man's brain, only they are much smaller. Holloway explains that we occasionally see the same sort of thing—well formed but small brains—in micro-encephaly, a fairly common type of birth defect. Persons born with smaller-than-normal brains are different from others in only one major way. They are less intelligent.

The first bits of accumulating anthropological evidence suggest that survival favored larger, stronger, and more intelligent humans. Conversely, nature gradually but steadily screened out smaller, weaker, less intelligent humans.

There are some difficult pills to swallow in considering man's evolutionary history—difficult because they run counter to currently accepted notions of morality.

One unpopular premise is that man's evolutionary development has probably been accelerated by his genocidal temperament. It now seems likely that Homo sapiens evolved most rapidly where competition for survival was most intense. The more frequently the strong killed the weak, the more each succeeding generation improved. The genetic characteristics of the stronger were transmitted with increasing reliability.

Another notion, unpopular but probable, is that man's evolutionary development was accelerated by polygamy. As with many other mammals, when the most powerful, intelligent males contribute more than their mathematical share of offspring, each succeeding generation is likely to be a bit stronger. Sexual appetite, like height and strength, is probably distributed on a normal curve. It may well be greater in men who ascend to alpha positions. Tribal leaders, until recent times, had more and easier access to females, and so passed on their genetic traits to relatively larger numbers of offspring.

Disease may have been as powerful a force in upgrading the quality of each succeeding generation as polygamy and man's warlike nature. As late as 3,000 years ago, the Old Testament describes how the Israelites feared contact with strange peoples of other tribes because the result was sometimes plagues, sickness, and disease. Here, as with war, men in regions which allowed or forced interaction among many tribes were more exposed to contagious diseases than men who were isolated by such geographical barriers as oceans, mountains or dense jungles.

Just as insects which survive pesticides may transmit resistant traits to succeeding generations, so also did people who survived plagues and diseases transmit their traits of greater immunity to succeeding generations. This suggests that when two peoples meet, those who are least immune are more likely to die from disease. Often the disease is carried and transmitted by those who are most immune due to a history of much tribal interaction.

It seems that the principles of survival of the fittest operate on a level of microbes, and could probably not be halted even if mankind practiced the morality he espoused and stopped killing off his weaker brothers and sisters.

Anthropology is the real history. And the perspective it yields tends to clarify that humans, like all living things around us, are changing. We are evolving. Our mastery of our environment, our knowledge of it and our ability to understand it, are improving. We are becoming more intelligent and more resistant to disease. Our chances for survival are improving.

Gloom and Doom Prophets

If our chances for survival are improving, why is modern man surrounded by so many gloomy prophets? They predict the disappearance of natural resources, and destruction of the protective layer of atmosphere which shields us from harmful solar rays. They predict over-population, famine, starvation, nuclear wars and disintegration of technological societies.

Nuclear weapons continue to proliferate. In 1974, India became the sixth nation to explode a nuclear bomb, and other countries will undoubtedly gain the capability of destroying the technological world.

With so much dependence on machines, what will happen to industrialized societies if the supply of petroleum-based fuels slows to a dribble?

Will abandoned cars dot the landscape like the dead buffaloes which preceded the decline of the Cheyenne? If alternatives to petroleum-based fuels cannot be rapidly developed, technology and all its new institutions may undergo a serious retrenchment.

And if neither the bomb nor the disappearing oil reserves destroys technological nations, the problem of overpopulation is there.

In *The Naked Ape*, Desmond Morris[62] calculated that if the current rate of increase in world population continues for another 260 years, there will be 11,000 individuals for every square mile of land surface.

Discussions of the future of technology should do some homage to Alvin Toffler. But *Future Shock*,[63] his best-known book, was clearly gloomy.

I wish he had ended his forecasts with this optimistic statement from page 282:

> *"We have reached a dialectical turning point in the technological development of society. And technology, far from restricting our individuality, will multiply our choices—and our freedom—exponentially."*

Instead, he predicts a new form of mental illness, "future shock," will emerge as a result of the enormous changes modern man must face. But some of his advice seems a bit hypochondriacal. He encourages us to pay close attention to heart palpitations, nervous tremors, insomnia, irritability and fatigue. And he suggests that we "close doors, wear sunglasses, avoid smelly places and shy away from strange surfaces." Weird!

So far, we are not discovering large numbers of people sitting at the foot of stairs, dazed, glassy-eyed expressions on their faces. Where is this future shock disease appearing?

It all sounds so ominous, this great plague, about to strike thousands. One pictures Marcus Welby with his most sincere expression:

"I'm afraid your son is suffering from future shock, Ruth. tell me, has he been around any smelly places lately?"

Ruth, with hurt, anxious expression: "he has been a little irritable."

Welby, with his famous fatherly tone: "Have him wear these sunglasses, and try to keep the doors in your house closed."

To the contrary, much current evidence suggests that people are becoming more healthy. We live longer. The resident populations of mental hospitals have been steadily declining for the past twenty years.

Toffler exaggerates the dangers of overstimulation. Richness and variety of stimulation are healthy rather than something to be feared. Why do human beings listen to music, travel, solve puzzles and spend millions of hours piddling around with balls—large ones, small ones, oblong ones—putting them in holes, through hoops, across goal lines, over nets? None of these activities appear to contribute directly to our survival. Why do we expend such enormous amounts of energy eagerly searching for new forms of stimulation if we are, as Toffler suggests, near some psychological breaking point of over-stimulation? We do it because we enjoy it. It's good for us.

Few students of abnormal psychology are forecasting any major new form of mental illness brought on by the increasing complexity, volume, or variety of choices or stimulation. Luckily, Toffler was far more optimistic in his later books.

The acid heads are also making gloomy predictions about some cataclysmic end to modern civilization. Timothy Leary claims that while he was holed up in the mountains following his escape from a California prison, some Weathermen introduced him to an Indian chief. The chief told him of "the prophesies":

> *"That the white machine man would destroy themselves with greed. That the Indians would persevere and preserve the earth. That a young generation of whites would let their hair grow and return to the tribal wisdom and the brotherhood of all wild animals."*[64]

In his book, *Beyond Freedom and Dignity*, B. F. Skinner[65] sees the problems of the world getting more severe. For Skinner, the only hope for survival is a planned and controlled program for conditioning man into new forms of behavior.

Richard Barnett and Ronald Muller, authors of *Global Reach*,[66] seem disturbed about the emerging power of the new giant multinational corporations. They join the argument on the side of those who believe that industrialization will ruin the environment if growth is not limited. They propose more stringent government controls, at the local community level, to force corporations into taking better care of community resources, including air, water, raw materials, and labor.

The forecasts of famine, overpopulation and energy shortages that emerged from the Club of Rome only a few years ago are already proving to be overly pessimistic. Reduced birth rates and increased food production in many developing countries, as well as the recent oil glut, suggest that some of the gloom-and-doom prophets will have to search for other ways to alarm us.

There are also some credible optimists. In his book, *The Greening of America*,[67] Charles A. Reich predicted a non-violent revolution as the first TV conditioned generation—the flower children, pot smoking, stop-the-war long hairs—rise into positions of leadership within our modern institutions.

I find myself firmly in the camp of Konrad Lorenz.[68] He believes the process of evolution will eventually solve problems of political strife and warfare. Lorenz, like other scientists who study long-range evolutionary tends, believes the human animal is evolving away from aggressive, predatory roles—that we are becoming more intelligent and more ethical in our treatment of one another.

In every age, there have been prophets of doom. But all those, so far, (with the possible exception of Noah) who sent people scrambling to garage roofs and bomb shelters to avoid the end of the world, were wrong.

Darwin[69] indicated that "all organic beings are striving to increase at a high ratio and to seize on every unoccupied or less well occupied place in the economy of nature."

This principle can surely be applied to tribes of humans. Human tribes long ago occupied every habitable area of the earth. Since then they have been struggling, first to expand or protect their hunting area, then to expand or defend their farmland. A cluster of men and women in a corporation is a survival unit. The variety of corporations, their voracious search for new products and new markets, as well as their aggressive growth in the last 100 years, shows how diligently corporate survival is pursued.

Darwin also observed that the young perish in the greatest numbers, then the old and feeble. There is a much higher failure rate in young businesses than among more mature corporations.

Each corporate entity struggles for survival within a given environment. Slight changes which favor some tribes are fatal to others.

*   *   *

When Congress withdrew the tax credit for new capital equipment in the late 1960s, I happened to be consulting for a small design engineering firm. Their products included huge sheet metal processing equipment. The various lines would trim, anneal, or pickle large rolls of sheet metal. The change in tax credit, a subtle environmental influence for most companies, provided a staggering shock for my client. For a while, the organization struggled to feed itself. But reduced sales did not provide sufficient nourishment. When it became difficult to meet the payroll, a series of staff reductions was made. The tribe dwindled in size. Even this did not help. Like the young or weak members of a deer herd in Africa, this struggling company fell prey to a predator, a hungry conglomerate.

*   *   *

But the overall picture of corporate survival is far from grim. Corporate failures do not result in the death or slaughter of employees. After a few months of searching, most people find new and sometimes better positions. Rapid growth in the number and size of corporations suggests that they are attuned to the new world environment. In fact, they are rapidly improving it.

Over the past ten years, high technology companies have undergone dramatic growth. The environment is right for computers. They are on the cutting edge of technological growth. Modern technology is providing a rich medium of growth for many machine-producing corporate tribes. The result is flourishing corporations.

Corporations, in common with all other tribes, be they hunting-gathering, pastoral or agrarian, strive for survival. Survival and growth, now as always, is the prime motive for all their plans and programs.

The capitalist chiefs of the corporate tribes follow no new or special creed. They are guided by the same survival and competitive motives that energized the chiefs of all the tribes that went before them.

Most modern men-of-knowledge would agree that Darwin was a visionary. He was skeptical of those who explained major changes in nature on the basis of dramatic or catastrophic events. He believed that the processes of growth and decline were not sudden. Darwin emphasized that evolutionary changes resulted from slight, selective changes which accrued over many generations, like compound interest. If his theories still apply, the most prudent and parsimonious forecasts of the survival of technology, and its corporate tribal units, is that they will continue their recent rate of growth. Time and time again, those prophets who said "the sun will rise tomorrow" have been correct.

What Every Marxist Needs to Know
About Corporations

When Darwin traveled around South America on his famous voyage aboard the H.M.S. Beagle, he visited the gold mines at Yaquil. In charge was an American gentleman named Nixon.

Darwin recorded the following entry in his journal on September 13, 1834—about one hundred and fifty years ago:[70]

"When we arrived at the mine, I was struck by the pale appearance of many of the men, and inquired from Mr. Nixon respecting their condition. The mine is 450 feet deep, and each man brings up about 200 pounds weight of stone. With this load they have to climb in a zigzag line up the shaft. Even beardless young men, eighteen and twenty years old, with little muscular development of their bodies (they are quite naked excepting drawers), ascend with this great load from

*nearly the same depth. A strong man, who is not accustomed
to this labour, perspires most profusely, with merely carrying
up his own body. With this severe labour, they live entirely
on boiled beans and bread. They would prefer having bread
alone; but their masters, finding they cannot work so hard
upon this, treat them like horses, and make them eat the
beans. Their pay is here . . . twenty-four to twenty-eight
shillings per month. They leave the mines only once in three
weeks; when they stay with their families for two days. One
of the rules in this mine sounds very harsh, but answers pretty
well for the master. The only method for stealing gold is to
secrete pieces of the ore, and take them out as occasion may
offer. Whenever the major-domo finds a lump thus hidden,
its full value is stopped out of the wages of all men; who
thus, without they all combine, are obliged to keep watch over
each other."*

Darwin, the great man-of-knowledge who unlocked the concept of evolution, probably did not realize that he was observing
a new tribal mutation—something that in a few generations
would dramatically change mankind. He did not know that in
less than 100 years, men and women all over the world would
lay down their native garments, migrate from their country
villages and take upon themselves the hard hat and double-
breasted regalia of the corporate tribesman.

Perhaps he did not recognize the tribal embryo because it
was so much like the agricultural tribes of his day. England
and most European countries were already rapidly converting
their farm populations into corporate work forces, and the earliest labor-intensive industries treated their workers much like
the peasants, serfs, servants, and slaves of the agricultural era.

There is little doubt that corporations have evolved a great
deal since Darwin made his observations. Working conditions
similar to those which Darwin described were not unusual in
the first pre-technological corporations. Without machines, management relied on the same kind of power that was used to
build the pyramids—manpower.

Under these conditions, work was painful. The first foremen and supervisors were strong men who applied steady pressure in order to achieve production targets. When pressure was relaxed, workers would relax and production would fall. The earliest work groups were made up of slaves, people detached from their territory by conquest. The earliest corporations resembled agricultural serfdoms. They relied on the efforts of a poor and uneducated laboring class. The company-owned mining towns which provided housing, jobs and credit at a company-owned store, were early expressions of the transition from agriculture to technology. They were corporate serfdoms.

Fifty years after Darwin's observations in Chile, Karl Marx wrote of children workers in Lancashire manufacturing districts.[71]

> *"They were harassed to the brink of death by excess of labour . . . were flogged, fettered, and tortured in the most exquisite refinement of cruelty; . . . they were in many cases starved to the bone while flogged to their work and . . . even in some instances . . . were driven to commit suicide."*

Workers in early corporate factories were displaced sharecroppers, immigrants and converted farm laborers. The socioeconomic class structure of the agricultural age was translated into and absorbed by early corporations. Those who owned the corporations differed from the hourly workers substantially, not only in wealth, but in education and political influence.

Marx and Engels were impressed by Darwin's theories. They recognized the emergence of the capitalists, the power and influence of the bourgeoisie, and the emerging threat of corporations to the sovereignty of nation states.

Marx was violently opposed to the exploitation, poverty, and horrendous working conditions he observed in the first emerging corporations. Early capitalists obviously adopted the values of feudal landowners of the agricultural era. Their workers were treated like slaves. They were clearly exploited by those with capital and hereditary wealth.

*   *   *

Jim Williams got his pink slip on Friday morning when he reported for work. There were ten others who, like himself, had lost their jobs. "It's nothing personal, Jim," the plant personnel man told him. "We have closed down the line you are working on. Our plant in Ohio can produce all the widgets we need."

To Jim it was extremely personal. He had worked hard. He had been loyal to XYZ Corporation and conscientious about his job.

Traffic was thin as Jim drove home from the plant. He was anxious to tell his wife while the children were still in school. But when he arrived home, she was not there—probably at the grocery store. He sat alone in the quiet house and wondered what he would do. He thought about the house payments, the car payments. Would he ever be in a position to send his children to college?

Two days later, XYZ declared its last quarterly dividend for the fiscal year. Larkin Bentworth, III, was pleased. His father, who founded the company, would have been pleased too. Larkin's total dividends for the fiscal year amounted to $15 million. Perhaps he would give his alma mater the money they needed to start construction on the new Bentworth Building.

Jim and Larkin were born six miles apart, and worlds apart. Jim's parents were poor, Larkin's were rich.

*   *   *

Some corporation owners still maintain attitudes of "divine right" and authoritarian management values that should make those who truly believe in democracy blush. However, even though the distance between the workers and principal stockholders in large corporations is often immense, conditions for a violent revolution—the workers rising up to wipe out management—which may have been ripening in Marx's lifetime, have long since passed in most industrialized nations.

Those conditions, which Marx regarded as inevitable, passed with the introduction of machines and the elimination of painful labor. Workers at all levels in modern corporate tribes recognize their improved standard of living and want it to continue.

The long, bitter struggles of trade unions, while not as violent as Marx predicted, have nonetheless helped to raise the standard of living and improve working conditions for millions of workers. If anger and resentment could be measured, the amount generated in millions of contract negotiations since Marx and Engels would be substantial, but this does not appear to be leading to the inevitable violent revolution Marx predicted. As in so many other areas of competition within corporations, the endless fight between management and labor is largely bloodless.

As governments of industrialized nations have become aware of the exploitation of the poor by the rich, they have instituted laws, regulations, and controls that have helped to ease the suffering of the poor. Governments have imposed laws against slavery, child labor and unsafe working conditions. We now have minimum wage and social security laws, laws against monopolies which suppress competition, laws against unfair labor and bargaining activities, laws against unfair hiring practices. Through such legislation, the exploitation of workers has clearly been modified. Graduated income, capital gains and inheritance taxes, have also helped to assure that the wealthy give a proportionally larger share to finance government services and social programs.

Corporate policies against nepotism, and the trend toward widely held public ownership of corporate stock, are also clear evidence of evolutionary changes away from conditions that used to separate men into more rigid socioeconomic classes.

Many of the things Marx struggled for seem to be emerging naturally as evolution takes its course. It is ironic that the modern bourgeoisie has led the way to a better life, better health, better education and a higher standard of living for everyone—not just shareholders and top executives.

The boundaries which separated men into classes in the age of Darwin and Marx are showing increasing signs of permeability among modern industrialized nations. Thousands of common men and women from poor and humble beginnings have risen to positions of wealth and influence within corporations.

Inherited wealth can still guarantee immense advantages in education, power, contacts and career opportunities. Inequities between life in the ghetto and Martha's Vineyard are still grossly unfair. Prisons are still filled with the poor, uneducated and unemployable. But the average working man in industrialized nations is less deprived, exploited or miserable than his predecessors. His standard of living is better than that of his parents and grandparents. Compared with the exploited proletariat Marx and Engels wanted to help, modern industrial workers live in paradise.

What every Marxist needs to know is that authoritarian, pyramid-shaped, dominance-ordered tribal structures are here to stay. They exist in every country, every working organization, no matter what political idealogy is espoused. Destroy them and new ones form.

Attempts to give control to the workers are naive. A ruling class or party can be thrown out, but a new dominance hierarchy will form. Soviet opposition to Polish workers demonstrate how the values and ideals espoused by Marx and Lenin have come full circle. Soviet leaders, like the tzars before them, must now control and dominate workers in order to maintain their perch at the top of the heap.

Class stratifications exist in every culture, including all communist and socialist countries. Marx, far from being a visionary or modern thinker, was attempting to hold back a river of evolution he did not fully understand. The early corporate tribes he so despised, and the capitalists who owned them, were the hope of the future.

The New World Tribes

So, as we have seen, corporations are emerging as new tribal forms. They are hybrids, mutations, the evolved food-getting survival units of technological man. No one planned it that way. One certainly cannot blame corporate leaders for it. It's just happening, evolving blindly, nourished by increasing technological development.

In the last 100 years corporations have been growing with amazing vitality. According to Edward R. Bagley in *Beyond the Conglomerates*,[72] there were about 1,700,000 corporations in the U.S. alone in 1974. The large ones are getting larger. Hundreds of new ones are struggling into existence in countries all over the world.

Hundreds of multi-national corporations are already firmly established. The first world tribes are rapidly taking form. Machine powered, bristling with health, they are growing larger, more powerful and more numerous each year. Their rapid growth, their power to alter ancient territorial bonds, to shift the population from its farming roots into cities, is evidence of their immense health.

The momentum of evolution is clearly in favor of continued growth of technology, of industrialization, of corporations. If Darwin's principles can be applied to corporate tribes, those which are large, which have survived the most severe industrial competition and which have developed the greatest variety and diversity of markets, will have the best chance for continued rapid growth.

Bagley shows that .0003 percent of the nation's 1,700,000 corporations—the 500 largest industrial corporations—account for 65% of all sales of U.S. industrial companies, 79% of total profits, and 76% of all employees.[73] Bagley predicts continued rapid economic growth, and emergence of super-corporations—highly diversified, fast growing, with at least a billion dollars of sales.

Corporations will do far more than survive. They will flourish. These giant conglomerates have worldwide employees, worldwide facilities, worldwide markets, worldwide labor pools, and make use of worldwide raw material sources.

Bagley regards Exxon, First National City Bank of Chicago, Gulf, Mobil, Texaco, Borden, Celanese, DuPont, W. R. Grace, Singer and Union Carbide as true multi-national corporations. All of the largest banks, public accounting, advertising and consulting firms have facilities and employees throughout the industrialized world.

Hundreds of large corporations now have multi-national organizations. They provide paychecks for citizens of many nations. They provide tax revenues for many nation–states. They transfer products, raw materials, money and employees from country to country. They rely on the manpower, markets and raw materials of many nations.

The book *Global Reach*,[74] by Richard J. Barnet and Ronald E. Muller, a well-researched study of multi-national corporations, presents convincing evidence of the power of the new world tribes. The facts it presents show clearly how effective the multi-nationals have been at converting resources from less-developed regions into corporate profits. They describe the rapid expansion of multi-nationals to take full advantage of foreign markets, raw materials, labor and capital.

The emergence of multi-national corporations may tend to blur traditional loyalties; citizens of several nation-states become tribesmen of the same corporation—European business leaders join forces to become the Common Market—foreign businessmen take ownership of companies in the U.S.. Nation-states increasingly find themselves competing to attract corporations, then dependent on them for new sources of tax revenues and jobs.

U.S. companies which close down manufacturing facilities here and open new ones in Taiwan are not so concerned about U.S. unemployment that they will sacrifice profits and growth for it.

When Kennecott cut back operations in its Bingham copper mine and increased output from Chile, it did so for its own corporate growth and survival. Its owners may assuage their concern for laying off Utah workers by the notion that they are providing jobs and upgrading living standards in Chile. Unlike Japanese corporations, which regard hard work and industrial growth as a patriotic mission, many U.S. corporations feel encumbered, picked on and abused by their own government. Patriotic motives take a back seat to profit motives.

Lessons from Allende

Salvador Allende's tragic story provides an example of the raw power of emerging world tribes.

Allende's hatred, frustration, and anger toward ITT and Kennecott in Chile prevented him from maintaining essential working relationships. He quarreled with them. He nationalized their plants and equipment. He slashed away at them, desperately trying to cut his country free from their influence, apparently not fully realizing he was cutting away at an economic umbilical cord. However small Chile's share of revenue from her own raw materials, it was essential. By angering and alienating powerful chiefs of multi-national tribes, Allende seriously damaged economic conditions within his own country. He needed parts, supplies and equipment from U.S. corporations. They were withheld or sold only for cash. His acts of nationalizing plants and equipment created a reflex response. He was deeply distrusted, and that had a direct impact on Chile's line of credit. Chile's borrowing power disintegrated almost overnight. Its line of short-term credit shrank from $220 million to $35 million in the first year of the Allende government.[75] The price of copper declined. The prices of Chile's imports rose.

In his speech to the United Nations on December 4, 1972, Allende explained what warfare with transnational corporate tribes is like.

> *"We find ourselves opposed by forces that operate in the shadows, without a flag, with powerful weapons that are*

*placed in a wide range of influential positions. . . . We are
the victims of almost invisible actions, usually concealed with
remarks and statements that pay lip service to respect of the
sovereignty and dignity of our country."*[76]

Sovereignty was easier to define when men were hunter-
gatherers and agriculturalists. It involved territorial boundaries—essentially geographical features of the earth.

Allende was the leader of a nation-state. He was doing battle
with corporate tribes. These were large, strong and diversified,
modern corporations. Their leaders were acquainted with other
corporate tribesmen throughout the world. Allende offended
them all when he took plants and equipment so abruptly. They
recoiled.

As Chile's economic conditions deteriorated, and the suffering of her citizens increased, Allende's fears proved to be more
than paranoid ravings. No armies had opposed him. No bombs
had fallen. The Chilean army had no adversary. In fact, Barnet
and Muller point out that Allende's military aid had actually
increased from $800,000 to more than $12 million in the first
two years of his rule.[77] His troops stood at the ready and watched
poverty increase about them as their country slid rapidly into
bankruptcy.

In Allende's attack on transnational corporations, he said,

*"We are faced by a direct confrontation between large
transnational corporations and the states. The corporations
are interferring in the fundamental political, economic and
military decisions of the states. The corporations are global
organizations that do not depend on any state and whose
activities are not controlled by, nor are they accountable to
any parliament or any other institution representative of the
collective interest. In short, all the world political structure
is being undermined. The dealers don't have a country."*[78]

Allende, like Marx, asserts that international corporations
weaken the nation states. Both are mistaken.

Drucker and others have correctly pointed out that nation-
states which have many large corporations have more, rather

than fewer, government employees. Government organizations have clearly evolved to provide control, guidance, regulations and laws which have often contributed to the healthy growth of their indigenous corporations.

Government organizations in technologically advanced nations often exist as products, or by-products, of corporate growth. In the U.S., the SEC, FAA, FDIC, EEOC, FCC—dozens of regulatory agencies—have arisen to exclusively regulate, control and serve corporations. These agencies exist solely to influence corporations, maintain fair play among and within them, provide contracts for them, tax them, settle disputes among them, encourage them to hire minority employees, make them safe for employees, and see that they restore the land and clean up their pollution. Armies of federal employees joust daily with armies of corporate employees.

The employed of the United States are 95% corporate tribespeople. It is not surprising that government organizations have become the customers, referees, rules makers, partners, employers, judges and servants of corporations.

Governing bodies of agricultural nation-states tended to serve the interests of their landowner constituents. The landowners provided both troops and tax revenues.

Governing bodies of nation-states are now serving the interests of their corporate constituents. The people are now largely corporate employees rather than farm workers. It is fitting that their representatives support their interests. Good government should contribute to the health and vitality of its indigenous corporate tribes.

Like Allende, the authors of *Global Reach* have also stated that the multi-national corporations have no territorial loyalties.[72] They are organizations which are "without a country." As world events unfold, it is becoming increasingly clear that even though multi-national corporations operate in, and use the resources of many nations, (including labor), they still identify strongly with their nation-states. Where there may be many multi-national corporations, there are relatively few multi-national boards of directors. In the U.S., only 1.6% of high-level executives of large multi-national corporations are non-Americans.

And when a serious threat to the territorial integrity of a nation-state emerges, as it did in World War II, corporations are quick to join in the defense. Just as the feudal lords of Europe sent troops, primarily farm workers, to fight wars, so also do corporate tribes send draft age men to fight against the enemy.

The freezing of Iranian assets in U.S. banks provides another graphic example of how the power of multi-national corporations can be mobilized in times of crisis. The unsheathing of this powerful financial sword was a clear example to the world that the U.S. was willing and able to use its power as a world banker to respond to threats. It was also a clear reminder to all foreign governments that peaceful, businesslike relationships must be maintained. Nation-states that threaten to nationalize U.S.-owned plants many risk the loss of their investments in U.S. properties.

Most multi-national corporations require peaceful world conditions to obtain a reliable return on their investments. The Arabian oil barons who buy U.S. homes, hotels, corporations, and real estate, do so with an expectation of continuing peaceful working relationships. And god-kings, like Khomeini, who attempt to lead their people back into agricultural values and lifestyles, may be like Marx, swimming against the current of evolution. They cannot offer their people the fruits of industrialization without cooperative international working relationships. And once their people taste these fruits, they are unwilling to return to the past.

Perhaps Iran attempted to move too quickly into industrialization. Just as the U.S. revels in Bonanzaland, feeling comfortable with the romantic frontier values of its past, so also do the Iranians embrace and feel comfortable with the values of their past.

Leaders of some industrialized nation-states accused U.S. banks of over-reaching their territorial boundaries when foreign branches of U.S. banks froze Iranian assets. But their complaints were not so vociferous that they damaged cooperative working relationships. They needed U.S. markets and understood the bloodless ground rules of the new era of corporate tribes.

When Iran deposed the Shah and embraced Khomeini, it merely replaced one god-king with another. Both men believed God had ordained them. Even the desire to execute the old god-king is an example of the values of an age gone by. In some African tribes, such as the Dinka, to execute the chief who had lost power was standard practice. Happily, Africa is no longer quite so primitive, and most of these tribal customs are history.

Whether accomplished against a foreign corporation (as in Chile), or as a result of internal politics (as in England and France), nationalizing corporations is usually a step backward. Few government leaders are familiar enough with the day-to-day challenges and options of a given industry to make better decisions than experienced executives on the firing line. To nationalize corporations is to harness them in extraneous regulations and political encumbrances. It weakens management, retards corporate growth and restrains corporations from aggressively and creatively capturing a larger claim on the world's limited and increasingly shrinking resources. It delays the arrival of the improved lifestyles that comes from technological development.

Governments which recognize the implications of our new territorial situation should nourish their corporate tribes, help them to grow, provide legislation, policies and programs that keep them healthy and competitive in world trade.

Saudi Arabia's ability to gain control of its oil is a study which contrasts dramatically with Chile's experience under Allende. Writing in Forbes, James Cook[80] indicates:

> *"The oil companies, Aramco among them, lost control first of their ability to set prices and then of their ability to control*

production, and once that happened, ownership no longer meant very much."

There was no bloodshed associated with the shifting of power in Saudi Arabia. The Saudis were more comfortable and skillful with capitalist strategy than classical Marxists. The oil companies were sympathetic with Saudi's desire to industrialize, and Saudi needed American markets as much as control of the oil. These ideas contributed to mutually beneficial agreements. Saudi won back control of its own oil resources through a process of persuasion, discussion and diplomacy. They had an ancient advantage. The oil was on their territory. The U.S. oil companies could increase prices, get U.S. consumers to pay, and divert the consumer's anger and criticism to the Arabs.

Building additional channels of trade and communication will be mutually beneficial. It will continue Saudi's accelerating technological development and improved living conditions. General Motors will export more Cadillacs. Thousands of `American workers will take home millions of dollars in paychecks, made possible by the purchase of equipment. Booz-Allen and McKinsey will get some big consulting contracts. Zenith will export more TV sets. McCann-Erickson will get some fabulous new advertising campaigns. IBM will sell more computers. And the Saudi population will rapidly abandon its agricultural lifestyle to become city-dwelling corporate tribesmen.

It is significant that the Saudis have been able to maintain many of their values and religious beliefs. The change from tribal life to corporate life came swiftly. Their native costumes are an observable indication that their tribal values and religious beliefs are being absorbed, intact, into their modern corporations.

Unlike U.S. or European corporations which attracted workers from a variety of ethnic, racial and religious backgrounds, the Saudis are managing to build corporations with more homogeneous employee groups. Their organizations may benefit from the similar values and beliefs of their work force. Their corporations may be more tribelike than corporations in more heterogeneous cultures. As a result, they may be able to better focus and mobilize the efforts of their employees, generate stronger team spirit and be more effective competitors for survival.

The Emergence of Third World Corporate Tribes

Many corporations continue to operate in foreign countries with methods, work rules, pay and working conditions which have become illegal back home.

In ways, we still permit corporations a degree of exploitation of peoples and resources of developing nations that we would find unconscionable at home.

Exploitation of underdeveloped nations by corporations emerged as a simple extension of colonialism. But when modern governments recognized exploitation of their poor, laws were enacted. Perhaps one reason industrialized nations permit the exploitation of workers in underdeveloped nations is that they are not present to witness it. In our indifference, we still allow some corporations to fill their shareholder's coffers with the fruits of near-slave labor.

Perhaps live television coverage of working conditions within mines, factories and production operations of large corporations which operate in underdeveloped countries would foster attitudes which could correct this unfortunate situation.

Corporations search out pockets of cheap foreign labor, just as they seek locations within the U.S. which offer it. Small towns and Chambers of Commerce compete with one another to make their industrial parks attractive for new corporate facilities.

Large corporations usually offer higher wages and better fringe benefits than smaller business entities in the cheap labor pockets. They upset the wage market and are often able to fill their labor requirements at the expense of smaller operations which must then keep pace with big corporation wages.

Thus the pockets for cheap labor within the U.S. are steadily filled, and corporations, like water, flow to areas where resources, including labor, give them the best growth potential.

Corporations in search of cheap labor, raw materials, markets and products, long ago recognized the world as their base of operation. Thus, leather is shipped from Chicago to Taiwan to be made into baseball gloves, then shipped back to the U.S. for sale—all made economical by the difference between Taiwan and U.S. wages.

In the book *Global Reach*, Barnet and Muller remind us that in Hong Kong, "60% of male workers work seven days a week for about a $1.00 a day."[81]

This worldwide search for cheap labor is a dynamic model which will eventually begin to fill these pockets around the world and actively stimulate third-world development and industrialization.

Multi-national corporations already have stockholders from many nation-states. The workers of the world should have a share of ownership in their multi-national corporate tribes. Their fortunes should grow with that of their corporations.

One obvious method for accelerating the pace of worldwide industrialization is to extend labor laws and stock purchase programs to include employees in foreign nations.

Socialist and Marxist regimes may think twice about nationalizing corporations if many of their citizens hold stock in them. If foreign employees are relying on stock holdings as a form of retirement income, they may resent government intrusion.

If *all* employees of multinational corporations are shareholders, these new world tribes may enhance their growing sovereignty. They may also stand as a barrier to the warring elements of nation–states. Such disruptions threaten, rather than protect or increase the odds for the growth and survival of modern multi-national corporate tribes.

As more developing countries become sophisticated in the ways of corporate tribes, the pecking order of world power will be realigned. The third-world countries will gradually regain control of their own raw materials, capital markets and labor. And the new corporations that can gain a lever will exploit it as aggressively as all the tribes that went before them. As this occurs, corporations in the industrialized nations can expect increasing competition.

The developing countries are well aware that their resources and labor have been used to create massive wealth for the owners and chiefs of multi-national tribes. Interest rates which would have been called "usury" a few years ago now drain the vitality of many developing nations, while yielding record profits to large banks.

The third world has a right to be angry. Its countries want and need their turn at the trough. But they must be careful not to kill the host, not to drain so much blood from the industrialized beasts as to cause illness or weakness, because the fastest and most reliable path to world prosperity is a robust world economy.

The shock wave of technology has already been felt worldwide, and unless something happens to curb the current trend, the process of industrialization will continue to sweep through the emerging nations. The worldwide population of farmers will continue its rapid decline, just as the hunters declined before them. Corporations are steadily replacing farms as the primary food getting entities of the new world.

Just as the U.S. farm population was absorbed by corporations, so also will corporations in developing countries throughout the world help with the problem of retraining and relocating their displaced farm populations.

Since the third world countries are much in need of capital to finance their entry into the industrialized community, their desire for a healthy world economy should be as great, if not greater, than that of developed countries. Events which threaten the supply of oil or capital have a more dramatic impact on third world nations than on those which are already industrialized. Thus, Argentina's misguided effort to expand its agricultural land by attempting to capture the Falkland Islands may slow down its active participation in the world economy. Disruptions in the fragile world economy are more devastating to the newer, younger industrial organizations than to mature ones. Just as a dry season, when the grass is thin, takes the heaviest toll on the newborn herbivores, so also will recessions and wars be more devastating to the emerging industries of the third world than to corporations which are mature.

In this context, OPEC's dramatic increases in the price of oil, and the U.S.'s retaliatory increases in interest rates, may represent greater threats to developing countries than to those which were already industrialized. The increased wealth of OPEC nations and U.S. banks is being paid for not only by industrialized nations, but also by the retarded growth of smaller developing nations.

It is becoming clear that the worldwide growth of industry may promote international cooperation as never before. As modern corporations recognize their interdependence, new cooperative goals will emerge. Relationships will become conducive to mutual growth. It is in everyone's interest to have healthy and growing corporations.

Developing nations are eager for industrialization. They see clearly the improved standard of living it creates. Many are angry at the United States and other technologically advanced nations only because they are on the wrong side of the "have, have-not" formula. Their bright young students come to the U.S. and Europe to study. They stay. Technology feeds itself with talent from many nations.

Modern corporations, particularly large ones, actively contribute to the worldwide expansion of technology. The governments of developing nations need large corporations. They need capital, know-how and successful long-term working relationships. As their industrialization advances and they are able to compete effectively in world markets, they can expect to gain the benefits enjoyed by industrialized nations.

Simply stated, the power and influence of modern multinational corporations is immense. Their role in stimulating worldwide evolution toward technological advancement and industrialization is one of leadership. Many corporations are stronger than developing nations. They cannot be conquered with troops. They conquer without troops. The bloody methods of the agricultural era are giving away to economic forms of competition.

Corporate Tribes and War

In the long view, corporations may be just beginning to emerge. As they grow, institutions of the agricultural world will change and fade, just as the hunter-gatherer institutions faded before them. The process is furthest advanced in countries with the greatest industrialization.

The new world tribes will compete aggressively for profits, for shares of world markets and resources. And as trade relations grow stronger, as international travel becomes cheaper, as the world shrinks, war will become an increasingly unattractive option. It will gradually fade away as world trade and more super-corporations emerge.

Man's most dangerous predator has always been other men. At first he killed for hunting territory. Then, for crop territory. The strong slaughtered the weak. The frequency of these wars was greatest on larger continents where many tribes competed for prime territory. Through the early deaths of hundreds of weaker generations, super-aggressive, super-intelligent hordes evolved.

The hunting and predatory instincts of primitive man still smolder in the carnivorous recesses of our brains. The creation of machines for war—ships, planes, rockets, defense systems— still provides a purpose for hundreds of thousands of machine men. So much so, that a cutback in the production of war machines seriously influenced the U.S. economy in the early 1970s and created massive unemployment in Seattle and San Diego.

Aircraft carriers are predatory machines—floating war cities with an atomic striking force capable of destroying entire nations. The aircraft carrier is a floating steel castle teeming with warriors, humming with the chorus of a thousand throbbing machines. In spite of evidence which suggests the vulnerability of aircraft carriers to attack from guided missiles, new ones are under construction for the Navy.

But machines are changing war. They have eliminated most face-to-face confrontations. The machine man seldom sees the enemy he kills. He delivers explosions with machines, and, in turn, is blown apart without seeing his adversary.

Nuclear bombs have changed the basic logic of war. When many nations can destroy the entire industrialized world, war seems senseless. Nuclear bombs might have ended the Korean or Vietnam conflicts, but were not used.

Until the A-bomb, the most powerful men remained reasonably safe in war. In meetings, generals treated one another as gentlemen. One is somehow jarred to read about opposing generals drinking tea and discussing their situation after thousands of their less privileged countrymen had been slammed together the day before, losing arms, legs and lives.

After feeding thousands of his countrymen to the cannons and leaving a trail of carnage and destruction throughout Europe, Napoleon lost only prestige and power at Waterloo. He retired to a villa on the Isle of Elba.

Is war merely a pastime for powerful men? Is it still true that the poor and uneducated masses are used as cannon fodder by those with power? In Vietnam, a high percentage of U.S. casualties were members of minority groups.

Recognizing that war has always been fought by rules—a sort of etiquette—may help us to understand why the atomic and hydrogen bombs may end war. They endanger the lives and possessions of the ruling leaders. They leave nothing of value to capture, and may touch off destruction of one's own fortune, which for corporate tribesmen is partially measured in corporate assets.

War hurts corporate survival by inhibiting trade relations and disrupting the emerging world economy. Non-atomic brush-fire wars on some out-of-the-way territory like Vietnam or the Falkland Islands are apparently still O.K. They give the generals what they want—an arena for doing their things. Aircraft carriers are ideal for predatory campaigns on the soil of third world nations.

Generals in every nation need war for fulfillment. Their purpose is directing war. Their dream of glory is to win a battle. The officer with combat experience gets promoted faster. Some career military men yearn for war experience to bolster their chances for advancement. For meaning, they need an enemy, a crisis. For public support, they need a fear of attack, suspicion of the intentions of foreign generals. Our modern warriors stimulate the arms race, the communist paranoia, the endless hackneyed claims that God is on our side and the devil is influencing the enemy. The general still beams in the glow of a million saluting troops, and still relishes the massive ego trip of commanding and directing the battle.

For the first time in history, the man on the street is TV educated—far better educated than Napoleon's cannon fodder, or for that matter, any other group of warriors in history. Many are able and willing to draw their own conclusions about threats to national security. They wonder, was it Vietnam's navy or its air force that most threatened the security of the United States? The idea is ridiculous. I can hear it now: "CBS reports an armada of junks off the coast of California."

Is it Nicaragua's air force, army or navy which most threatens the security of the United States?

Unable to believe that events in Vietnam threatened the security of their country, many were unwilling to kill or to die for the cause. *Was* there a cause, aside from the aggrandizement of the military, a chance to pull the trigger on those fantastic new multi-million dollar war machines?

Mass education undermines the blind obedience of the masses. Live television coverage of war makes it difficult to believe in the heroic poses and clear-eyed determination of statues on war memorials in places like downtown Indianapolis. Live television coverage reveals that war is not glorious. The image John Wayne gave us is a tragic Hollywood fantasy. Live TV coverage of combat educates the folks back home to the unglorious, unromantic reality of war. It disturbs them, makes them question more than ever before the tradition of blind obedience to the whims of militant leaders.

Just as most of us operate with deeply entrenched stereotypes of our corporate roles, so also do we respond to ancient archetypes regarding our perceived enemies. Our tribal heroes may require an enemy archetype for meaning. Do our national leaders, in order to go down in history as heroes, need an enemy, someone to focus our tribal hatred? Do we need an evil enemy to help us believe in our own basic virtue and goodness?

When one considers all the "enemy" labels created in man's history of wars and conflicts—terms such as redcoats, rebels, japs, reds, gerries, gooks, charlie, infidels, gentiles and heathens—it seems as if we may need the concept of "enemy" to satisfy some aspect of our national self-image. Every few years we seem to apply our stereotype of the enemy to whatever nation is perceived as the greatest threat. That nation takes on all the descriptive adjectives of our ancient enemy stereotype.

It seems strange that we were able to refocus our hatred of Germany and Japan on Russia so quickly and completely after World War II. Can Reagan fulfill his heroic dream without people like Castro? Can Castro be a hero without the U.S. to serve as a focus for Cuban hatred?

In the U.S., all that seems necessary to focus our national hatred and mobilize the powerful enemy archetype is to apply the label "communist". We tend to forget how many nations we have considered godless, evil, immoral or untrustworthy since our own nation was founded only 200 years ago.

Our opposition to the USSR, Cuba, North Korea, and now Nicaragua may help these nations consolidate and strengthen their internal unity and resolve. Perhaps "communism", by providing an external focus for our "enemy" archetype, removes attention and support from internal revolutionary movements.

The principle can also be applied to corporations. When competitors are clearly and frequently defined, when corporations struggle mightily for market share against well known adversaries, the urgency and frequency of internal conflicts may ease. Conversely, corporations which are not clearly focused on economic war with external competitors may be allowing innate remnants of tribal aggression to focus internally, causing labor disputes, competition between departments and struggles for power and territory among ambitious executives.

I worry about all the aircraft carriers, planes and missile silos—so many nuclear bombs aimed at so many cities. Is there one buried somewhere in a silo in Siberia aimed at my home city? I worry about the armies of spies, agents, intelligence, counter-intelligence, all the espionage, the endless and growing cops-and-robbers games at the public's inconvenience and expense.

These are the largest and most dangerous threats to survival and world peace. Some Soviet general or CIA leader, believing with all his heart that he is saving his country, could easily create the next war.

Benevolent Corporations

Studies of the relatively advanced agricultural civilizations of the Aztecs and Mayans reveal that human sacrifice, as well as cannibalism, was widespread. These revelations underline how far industrialized nations have evolved toward more humane and compassionate values. As recently as 500 years ago, late in the 10,000-year era of agriculture, some authorities estimated that the Aztecs sacrificed as many as 250,000 persons per year, about 1% of their population.[82]

In Mayan and Aztec civilizations, the scarcity of game, lack of domesticated animals, and increasing population density created a serious lack of protein. There is little doubt that victims of the grisly cut-out-the-heart ceremonies were butchered and eaten by nobles following sacrificial rites. A prime objective of Aztec armies was to capture human meat.

The cruel machines for torture observed in places like the dungeon of Warwick castle in England were in operation only a few hundred years ago.

In terms of benevolent ideals, corporations are clearly a refinement over earlier tribal forms. There is very little violence within corporations. No corporations apply torture or physical punishment to employees who break the rules. Corporations may fire workers, disappoint them, use them and abuse them, but no blood is shed.

The public accounting profession, pummelled and picked on though it may be, greatly facilitates trust among corporations. Billions of dollars change hands daily on the basis of agreements between one company and another. One agrees to buy something from another. They specify the price, the quantity, the delivery date. A deal is made, credit extended, checks written, all based on trust, on a tradition of honesty and dependability we take for granted.

American Indian tribes seeking rapid growth would occasionally put on war paint and attack their neighbors. They would normally execute as many adult males as they could catch, and absorb the women and children into their own tribes as slaves, wives or adopted children.

Modern corporations do the same thing, bloodlessly. We call it an acquisition. It is not unusual that top executives of an acquired corporation are symbolically put to the sword. But no real blood is shed.

Corporations do not physically attack one another. Unlike the mafia, they employ no hit men. They sanction no slavery. Employees can and often do change companies if they do not like working conditions or pay.

An understanding of the history of evolving human tribes helps in recognizing that corporations have come a long way in developing humanistic organizations. They have instituted methods for survival that are relatively free from violence and bloodshed.

Those who attack corporations, who complain about the boredom, fear or lack of challenge within them, should study the full multi-million year range of tribal evolution. Only when the real anthropological perspective is understood can we begin to recognize the emergence of new, more humane, less violent tribes.

The new tribes are corporations. They are aggressive. They compete. They struggle as ruthlessly for survival and growth as all the tribes that preceded them. But they generally play by agreed upon rules. They do not sanction torture or require human sacrifice. The worst punishment they deliver is firing— banishment. And although fired employees are hurt and inconvenienced, most are able to continue their careers with new companies. No one is killed. The vast majority of these new tribes pay their bills on time. They can normally be trusted. The leadership, with all its riches in terms of dividends, stock options, bonus awards and executive perquisites, passes from one generation to the next with surprising smoothness.

Of course, there are arguments, there are strategic duels for power, there are intense competitive struggles for dominance. There are winners and losers. But the days of tribes slaughtering tribes, of murder and internal violence for control of power are fading. Those conditions may still exist in emerging nations which cling to traditions of their agricultural past, but those who join the hunt of the corporate tribesman will, in time, work for a healthy world economy, one without bloodshed.

We can no more imagine the full flowering of our technological civilization than could the first men to plant food, grow crops and domesticate animals have predicted the flowering of agricultural civilizations. The massive conversion of hunting grounds into crop land, the growth of cities, the emergence of armies, governments, and organized religions that blossomed in complex, yet parallel patterns throughout the earth, were clearly beyond the imaginative capacity of the first agricultural men.

And predictions of corporate destiny which attempt to use the 10,000-year era of agricultural history as a foundation for forecasting, without proper recognition of the changes in man's fundamental relationship to territory that resulted from the technological takeoff, must surely miss the mark.

Corporations may be only on the brink of greatness, of a time when life will be even more secure, more enjoyable, more free from the ghosts, curses, and irrational fears of the past.

Closing Remarks

We humans dwell together in clusters. We have always done so. Early men were pack-hunters. Women were gatherers. The human group was the tribe. This form of territorial adaptation was superseded by agriculture. Nations and armies arose. Just as Darwin predicted, these new tribal forms overran and exterminated the ones that had existed before. It was survival of the fittest. The Bible gives horrible evidence of how the largest and strongest tribes often slaughtered the weaker ones.

On the larger continental masses, where many tribal groups competed for crop land, men have fought to the death for generations to control territory. From those battles, intelligent, strong, aggressive, and tribally mixed hordes of farmer-soldiers emerged.

But the migration from farmland to cities has been bloodless. The farms remain, producing more crops than ever, but the population has shifted into new human clusters.

Corporations are the new clusters, the new food-getting teams of technological men and women. They are rapidly spreading throughout the world.

Corporations do not make bloody war on competitors. Presidents of corporations are rarely murdered, nor do they execute people they dislike. Slavery is almost gone. The uneducated masses are disappearing. Employees in corporate tribes are more safe from attack, physical pain or fear of supernatural dangers than members of any prior tribes in the history of mankind. The mythological ghosts and gods are also disappearing, replaced by a menagerie of modern TV heroes and heroines.

Few corporate employees spend a fraction of the survival effort their grandfathers spent. In fact, most physical effort now occurs in the context of play. Machines have helped create a paradise on earth. Today, ordinary corporate tribesmen enjoy luxuries in health care, food selection, communication, transportation and entertainment that czars, kings, and generals of past ages could never have imagined.

Cross-cultural comparisons indicate that the modern corporate employee has overcome many of the uncontrolled environmental threats that influenced the daily lives of primitive tribes-people. We need not struggle for food. We are relatively free of the ghosts, the angry gods, the demons, witches, and devils, that populated the thoughts of primitive tribesmen. We are relatively free from threats of conquest. Our understanding of disease, volcanoes, lightning, tornadoes, comets, eclipses and floods, though incomplete, at least provides us with enough understanding to drain off some of the irrational fears they produced in our ancestors.

Who will speculate about what General Motors, Exxon, and Bank of America will be like in another 100 years?

We tribesmen and tribeswomen are unconscious participants in a new birth, still infants, still emerging, partially unconscious of our new role in the world. We are the people of a new tribal mutation. We may be infinitely stronger in our ability to survive than anything that has gone before.

Continued growth of corporate tribes will probably have a positive impact on world peace. Eventually, bloody war, like cannibalism and slavery will be only an embarrassing reminder of our less human, more animal past. We will continue to fight for markets, raw materials, capital, labor, and for control of advertising space and air time. Some tribes will grow. Others will fail. Science will continue to increase our knowledge and mastery of our environment. Our survival chances will continue to improve. Darwin said it best with his wonderful simile of the tree to which I have referred earlier, and now quote:

> *"The affinities of all the beings of the same class have sometimes been represented by a great tree. I believe this simile largely speaks the truth. The green and budding twigs may represent existing species; and those produced during former years may represent the long succession of extinct species. At each period of growth all the growing twigs have tried to branch out on all sides, in the same manner as species and groups of species have at all times overmastered other species in the great battle for life. . . . Of the many twigs which flourished when the tree was a mere bush, only two or three, now grown into great branches, yet survive and bear the other branches; so with the species which lived during long-past geological periods, very few have left living and modified descendents. From the first growth of the tree, many a limb and branch has decayed and dropped off; and these fallen branches of various sizes may represent those whole orders, families, and genera which have now no living representatives, and which are known to us only in a fossil state. . . . As buds give rise by growth to fresh buds, and these, if vigorous, branch out and overtop on all sides many a feebler branch, so by generation I believe it has been with the great Tree of Life, which fills with its dead and broken branches the crust of the earth, and covers the surface with its ever-branching and beautiful ramifications."*[83]

BIBLIOGRAPHY

Chapter I
OUR TRIBAL NATURE

1. Freud, Sigmund *Totem and Taboo*, trans. James Strachey (New York: W. W. Norton & Co., Inc., 1950)

2. Jung, Carl G. *The Collected Works of Carl G. Jung*, (London, Routledge & Kegan. Paul; New York Pantheon, 1962)

3. Mehring, Franz *Karl Marx*, (New York: Covici, Friede, Inc., 1935).

4. Spencer, Herbert *The Principles of Sociology*, (New York: D. Appleton and Company, 1897).

5. Tiger, Lionel *Men In Groups*, (New York: Random House, Inc., 1969).

6. Jay, Antony *Corporation Man*, (New York: Random House, Inc., 1971).

7. Deal, Terrence E. & Kennedy, Allan A. *Corporate Cultures The Rites and Rituals of Corporate Life* (Reading, Massachusetts: Addison-Wesley Publishing Company, 1982).

8. Tiger, Lionel, *op. cit.*, page 78.

9. Crook, John Hurrel "Corporation in Primates," *Eugenics Review* 58, 2 (June 1966):68.

10. Malinowski, Bronislaw *Argonauts of the Western Pacific; An Account of Native Enterprise & Adventure in the Archipelagoes of Melanesian New Guinea*, pref. by Sir James G. Frasier (New York: E. P. Dutton & Co., Inc., 1961).

11. Goodall, Jane Van Lawick *In the Shadow of Man* (New York: Dell Publishing Co., Inc., 1971) p. 191.

12. Fox, Robin *Encounter with Anthropology* (New York: Dell Publishing Co., Inc., 1968) p. 88.

13. McLuhan, Marshall and Fiore, Quentin, *The Medium Is the Message* (New York: Bantam Books, Inc., 1967).

14. Tinbergen, N. *Social Behavior in Animals*, (New York: Wiley, 1953).

15. Ardrey, Robert *The Territorial Imperative* (New York: Dell Publishing Co., Inc., 1966).

16. Ardrey, Robert *op. cit.*, page 43.

17. Ardrey, Robert *op. cit.*, page 44.

18. Ardrey, Robert *op. cit.*, page 55.

19. Malinowski, Bronislaw *op. cit.*

20. Page, Martin *The Yam Factor* (New York: Doubleday, 1972).

21. A number of anthropologists have claimed that tribes they observed had no rulers or chiefs. For example, Colin M. Turnbull in *The Forest People, a study of the Pygmies of the Congo*, New York: Simon and Schuster, 1961) page 110, reported that there were no chiefs or formal counsels among the Pygmies. However, on page 107, in describing an incident where a hunter named Cephu had made a classic "end-run" during a communal hunt, setting his nets up ahead of the others, Cephu and the other tribesmen acknowledged that he was a chief of his own band.

In *NISA The Life and Words of a !Kung Woman*, Marjorie

Shostak reports that the "!Kung do not have status hierarchies or legitimized authorities such as chiefs or headmen." (Page 10). Yet on page 209, she reports that the subject of her book, NISA, lived in a village with a headman named Isak.

One of the central arguments of this book is that dominance hierarchies are a species specific phenomenon. The formality of the hierarchy may be less clear in some primitive hunting gathering groups, but it does exist. Hierarchies may become more formalized in societies that are more complex.

Some early anthropologists were probably misled into thinking there were no chiefs. In this way tribesmen insulated and protected their leaders. In Polynesia where eloquent men were often given honorary posts as "talking chiefs", anthropologists often mistook them for the real chiefs who gained their top status by birthright. Outside visitors, including visiting anthropologists, much to the amusement of the tribespeople, often courted and paid homage to the wrong man.

22. The term "man of knowledge" is from Carlos Castaneda, *The Teachings of Don Juan: A Yaqui Way of Knowledge* (New York: Simon and Schuster, 1968).

Chapter II
TRIBAL TERRITORY

23. Stanley, Henry M. *In Darkest Africa* (New York: Charles Scribner's Sons, 1890).

24. Morison, Samuel Eliot "Landfall," in *Essays*, ed: Leonard F. Dean (n.p.: Harcourt, Brace and Company, Inc., 1933), p.218.

25. Morison, Samuel Eliot, *op. cit.*, p. 219.

26. Levi-Strauss, Claude *From Honey to Ashes* (Science of Mythology Ser.), 1980. Reprint of 1973 ed. lib. bdg. 30.00X (ISBN 0-374-94952-2). Octagon.

27. Brown, Dee *Bury My Heart at Wounded Knee* (New York: Bantam, 1972).

28. Leakey, Richard E. and Lewin, Roger, *People of the Lake* (New York: Doubleday & Co., Inc., 1978, p. 207).

29. Frazier, Sir J. G., *The Golden Bough* (n.p.: The Macmillan Company, 1922).

30. Stewart, Kilton, *Pygmies and Dream Giants* (New York: W. W. Norton & Co., 1954, p. 217 and 64).

31. *The Holy Bible* Numbers Chapter 31 verse 35.

32. Youngblood, Ron *On the Hana Coast* (Honolulu: Emphasis International Ltd. and Link Inc. 1983) Page 41.

33. Formander, Abraham *Hawaiian Antiquities and Folk-lore* (Honolulu: Bernice P. Bishop Museum Memoirs. Vols. 4, 5, 1917, 1918.

34. Engels, Friedrich "The Origin of the Family, Private Property and the State; in *Handbook of Marxism* (New York: International Publishers, 1935) pp. 301-338.

35. Rostow, W. W. *Politics and the Stages of Growth* (London: Cambridge University Press, 1971).

36. Caughey, John L., "Media Mentors", *Psychology Today*, September, 1978).

37. Mead, Margaret, *Coming of Age in Samoa* (n.p.: William Morrow & Co., 1928).

38. Stanley, Henry M., op. cit.

39. McLuhan, Marshall and Fiore, Quentin, op. cit., p. 138.

Chapter III
ON THE EVOLUTION OF TRIBAL ROLES

40. Shostak, Marjorie, *NISA, The Life and Words of a !Kung Woman* (New York: Random House, Inc. 1981).

41. Spenser, Herbert, op. cit.

42. Freud, Sigmund, op. cit.

43. McClelland, David C. *Power: The Inner Experience* (New York: Irvington, 1975).

44. *Executive Compensation Service, The Corporation Directorship*, 6th ed. (New York: AMACOM, 1974) p. 17.

45. Ibid., p. 18.

46. Lamb, Bruce, *Wizard of the Upper Amazon*, 2nd ed. (Boston: Houghton Mifflin Co., 1975).

47. Castaneda, Carlos, *op. cit.*

48. Freud, Sigmund *op. cit.*

49. Berelson, Bernard and Steiner, Gary A., *Human Behavior: An Inventory of Scientific Findings* (New York: Harcourt, Brace & World, Inc., 1964).

50. Maziere, Francis, *Mysteries of Easter Island* (New York: Tower Publications, Inc., 1965).

Chapter IV
STRENGTHENING CORPORATE TRIBES

51. Ouchi, William, *Theory Z. How American Business Can Meet The Japanese Challenge* (Reading, Massachusetts, Addison-Wesley Publishing Company, Inc., 1981).

52. Turnbull, Colin, *The Mountain People* (New York: Simon and Schuster, 1972).

53. Nance, John, *The Gentle Tasady,* (New York: Harcourt, Brace, Jovanovich, 1975).

54. Deal, Terrence E. & Kennedy, Allen A. *op. cit.*

55. KQRS, "Native American Program," 16 March 1975, SCAN #11, "The Native American and Culture."

56. Deal, Terrence E. & Kennedy, Allen A., *op. cit.*

57. Peters, Thomas J. and Waterman, Robert H. Jr., *In Search of Excellence* (New York: Harper & Row, 1982).

58. Jay, Antony, *op. cit.*

59. Deal, Terrence E. & Kennedy, Allen A., *op. cit.*

60. Peters, Thomas J. and Waterman, Robert H. Jr., *op. cit.* p. 101.

Chapter V
ON THE EVOLUTION OF CORPORATE TRIBES

61. Holloway, "The Casts of Fossil Hominid Brains," *Scientific American* 231 (July 1974).

62. Morris, Demond, *The Naked Ape* (New York: Dell Publishing Co., Inc., 1967).

63. Toffler, Alvin, *Future Shock* (New York: Random House, Inc., 1970).

64. Leary, Timothy, *Confessions of a Hope Fiend* (New York: Bantam Books, Inc., 1973), p. 142.

65. Skinner, B. F., *Beyond Freedom and Dignity* (New York: A Bantam/Vintage Book published by arrangement with Alfred A. Knopf, Inc., 1972).

66. Barnet, Richard J. and Müller, Ronald E., *Global Reach* (New York: Simon & Schuster 1974).

67. Reich, Charles A., *The Greening of America* (New York: Random House, 1970).

68. Lorenz, Konrad, *On Aggression* (New York: Bantam Matrix Editions, 1963).

69. Darwin, Charles, *The Origin of Species by Means of Natural Selection* (New York: D. Appleton & Co., 1897).

70. Darwin, Charles, *The Voyage of H.M.S. Beagle* (New York: The Heritage Press), p. 240.

71. Mehring, Franz, *Karl Marx The Story of His Life* (New York: Covici Friede Publishers, 1935).

72. Bagley, Edward R., *Beyond the Conglomerates* (New York: D. Appleton and Company, 1897).

73. Ibid., p. 18.

74. Barnet, Richard J. and Müller, Ronald E., *op. cit.*

75. Ibid., p. 83.

76. *International Firms and Modern Imperialism*, Editor: Hugo Radice (Harmondsworth, Middlesex, England; Penguin Books Inc., 1975). p. 237.

77. Barnet, Richard J. and Müller, Ronald E., *op. cit.* p. 83.

78. *International Firms and Modern Imperialism, op. cit.* p. 242.

79. Barnet, Richard J. and Müller, Ronald E., *op. cit.*, p. 17.

80. Cook, James "Don't Blame the Oil Companies: Blame the State Department; How the West was Won", *Forbes* 117: 69-70 April 15, '76.

81. Barnet, Richard J. and Müller, Ronald E., *op. cit.* p. 22.

82. Horner, Michael, "The Enigma of Aztec Sacrifice", *Natural History*, April 1977, Pg. 47.

83. Darwin, Charles *The Origin of Species* (New York: D. Appleton and Company, 1897) Vol. 1, pp. 162-3.

INDEX

Abbott Laboratories, 36
accountants, 63
accounts receivable, 94
achievement motivation, 108
Achilles, 107
acquisitions, 196
adult role models, 76
advertising, 90
Africa, 107, 185
aggression and TV, 69
agricultural:
    era, 63
    family clusters, 75
    serfdoms, 175
    tribes, 16, 63
    tribesmen, 40
agriculture, 50, 56, 118
    age of, 58
agriculturists, 61
aircraft carriers, 192, 195
Akwaaba tribe, 37, 38
allegiance, 136

Allende, Salvador, 181, 182, 183
alpha, 12, 45, 102
    as profit maximizer, 127
Amacom, 112
Amazon, upper, 115
American Indians, 73
    ideas of nudity, 122
Anima, 11
animal clusters, 10
animal gods, 56
animal studies in zoos, 17
animism, 117
Animus, 11
anthropological time frame, 62
anthropology, 168
Archimedes, 117
archetypal roles, 45, 88, 127, 157
archetypes, 11
    enemy, 194
Ardrey, Robert, 24, 25, 27, 48
Argentina, 190
Aristotle, 117

armies, 59, 63, 79
    as vestigial organs, 80
assertiveness training, 159
assessment center, 28, 158, 159
Association of Humanist Psychologists
    (AHP), 41
athletics, 98
atomic bomb, 82, 192
attorneys, 63
Australian aborigines, 51, 140
Australopithecine, 166
automobile, 65
    evolution and the, 66
Aztecs, 195
        armies, 196

baboons, 24, 26, 102
Bagley, Edward R., 179, 180
banishment, 132
Bank of America, 199
bar mitzvah, 140
Barnett, Richard and Ronald Muller,
    170, 180, 182, 188
Berelson and Steiner, 118
Berlin Wall, 80
Beyond Freedom and Dignity, 170
Beyond the Conglomerates, 179
Bible, 198
Bingham copper mine, 181
birth order research, 107
blue collar workers, 163
board meetings, 144
Board of Directors, 12, 88, 112, 113
board room as an evolved council hut,
    112
Bonanzaland, 184
bonuses, 32, 156
Booz-Allen, 186
Borden, 18

Boy Scouts, 17
brain, 166
Brazil, 54
breeding in Kobs, 25
"bring home the bacon", 90
Brinkley, David, 71
Britain, 63
Buechness, Helmut K., 24

California Personality Inventory, 109
Camaroons, 140
Canary Islanders, 52
cannibalism, 79, 195
Caribbean, 122
carpet bombing, 81
Carson, Johnny, 71
Carter, Jimmy, 107
castles, 61
Castro, Fidel, 194
Catholicism, 124
Caughey, John L., 71
CBS, 67, 193
Celanese, 180
ceremonies, 19, 140, 142, 143, 152
    circumcision, 45
    infant naming, 19
    rites of passage, 89, 139, 140
    service award, 144
Chairman of the Board, 107
chambers of commerce, 187
changing companies, 130
Cheyenne, 54, 55
chief(s), 12, 101, 102, 104
    as supernatural, 103
    Executive Officer, 113
    in agricultural tribes, 106
    in corporate tribes, 107
    magnet for attention, 150

child labor, 177
child rearing, 21
  and grandparents, 77
children, 76
  become involuntary nomads, 77
  modern, 76
Chile, 175, 182, 185
Chimpanzee(s), 24
  families, 15
  females, 15
  males, 15
China, 63, 107
Christ, 63, 122
Christian missionaries, 121
church(es), 19, 63
  service as tribal experience, 142
  states, 62
cities, 63
clan groups, 153
class stratifications, 178
clerical workers as evolved gatherers,
  148
closing the sale, 91
Club of Rome, 171
collective unconscious, 11, 129
Columbus, 152
commencement, 20
  in high school, 140
commitment, 75, 129, 134, 135
  cradle-to-grave, 132
  reciprocal, 136
  shallow, 131, 134, 155
Common Market, 180
communications, 65
Communism, 195
Comparative Family Patterns, 15
compartmentalized life styles, 72
compensation, 32

computerized management information
  systems, 161
Congress, 70
consultants, 63, 148
consumer relations, 162
Control Data, 82
Cook, Captain James, 53, 59, 185
Cooperation in Primates, 13
Copernicus, 44
corporal punishment, 36
Corporate Cultures, 12, 139, 154, 162
Corporate Directorship, The, 112
corporate:
  employees, 83
  failures, 172
  hunters, 84
  logos, 154
  man, 86
  man-of-knowledge, 124
  management, 13
  nomads, 73
  presidents, 110
  presidents, personality characteristics
    of, 108
  pyramids, 135
  totems, 153
  tribe(s), 63, 75, 162
  tribe as a metaphor, 160
  tribesmen, 44, 74, 76, 162
Corporation Man, 12, 162
corporation(s), 16, 62, 64, 83, 133,
  150
  and bland commitment, 130
  and bloodshed, 35
  benevolent, 195
  do not attack, 196
  firings within, 110
  Japanese, 132, 158

like beehives, 129
modern, 140
multi-national, 179
not families, 163
on the brink of greatness, 198
replacing farms, 189
run by teams, 111
tribes, 162
council huts, 40
Council of Elders, 12, 31, 32, 45, 88,
107, 111, 112, 113, 144
cranial capacity, expansion of, 15
Crazy Horse, 107
Cronkite, Walter, 71
Crook, John Hurrel, 13
cropland, 51, 55, 61, 62, 63, 78, 79,
80, 82, 100, 198
Cuba, 194
culture, 162

Dalai Lama of Tibet, 107, 117
Darwin, 53, 87, 154, 171, 172, 173,
174, 175, 178, 179, 198, 200
Darwin's tree metaphor, 10, 200
deadwood, 138, 158
Deal and Kennedy, 12, 139, 154, 162
death blow, 91
developing countries, 189
Development Center, 158, 159
Dinka tribe of Africa, 185
"dipping one's pen in company ink",
153
divine rulers, 107
divorce rates, 77
dominance hierarchies, 11, 19, 45,
152
dominant males, 25, 102, 103
Drucker, 182
DuPont, 154, 180

Easter Island, 121
EEOC, 183
Egypt, 56, 59, 107
Einstein, 124
elders, 145
eldest sons, 107
Employee Stock Ownership Program
(ESOP), 155, 156
employee stock purchases, 148
England, 59, 185
Engles, 61, 175, 177, 178
entertainment and TV, 69
esprit-de-corps, 130
Eskimo, 51
Ethiopia, 107
evolving roles, 126
executives, 34
manufacturing, 92
women, 146
exercise programs, 159
exploitations:
of the poor, 177
of underdeveloped nations, 187
extended family relationships, 76
extended tribe, 71
Exxon, 180, 199

FAA, 183
factory worker, 12
Falkland Islands, 19, 193
families, 75
family(s):
emergence of, 16
government, 106
interaction, 68
metaphor, 163
relationships, 68
structure, 86

structure, changes in, 16
farm workers, 81
farmer-soldiers, 61, 62, 163, 198
father(s), 57
    role, emergence of, 16
Faust, 117
FCC, 183
FDIC, 183
"feeding the tribe", 90, 164
female:
    bonding, 95
    ceremonies, 95
    professional athletes, 99
fetisher(s), 116, 119
field sales, 98
file clerks, 12, 94
financial wizard(s), 45, 88, 125
firing, 134, 136
    threats of, 135
First National City Bank of Chicago, 180
Flying Tiger Line, 153, 154
food provider territory, 50, 51
football, 69
Forbes, 185
foreign ownership, 80
Fornander, Abraham, 60
Fortune's 500, 37
Fox, Robin, 15
France, 185
fraternities, 17
freezing of Iranian assets, 184
Freud, 12, 17, 103, 117, 154
funerals, 19
Future Shock, 169

gatherers, 12, 14, 93, 94
    in staff roles, 99

GE, 154
General Motors, 186, 199
generals, 106, 193
genetic transmission, 14, 24, 66
Germany, 194
"getting the ax", 132
Girl Scouts, 17
Global Reach, 170, 180, 183, 188
"global village, the", 20
God, 62, 117, 124, 125, 131
god-kings, 106, 110, 126
Goodall, Jane, 15, 26
gorillas, 102
Grace, W. R., 180
grandparents, 76
Great Wall of China, 80
Greece, 59
Greeks, 122
Greening of America, The, 171
Grenada, 19
grooming programs, 159
Gulf, 180

Haile Selassie, 107
Hallmark, 154
happy hunting ground, 50
Hawaii, 59, 60, 122
Hawaiian, 54
    volcanoes, 122
Hazda tribe, 54
head-hunting, 79, 105
    rituals, 92
head peckers, 21
headshrinker(s), 45, 88, 114, 125, 156
headquarters offices, 86
heaven, 124, 125
Hebrews, 107
Hellenes, 59

herd behavior, 9
high-powered attorney, 88
Hittite, 81
HMS Beagle, 53, 173
Holloway, Ralph, 165, 166
Hondas, 79
Hong Kong, 188
hoopla, 146
hourly workers, 33
human:
   clusters, 10
   evolution, 62
   sacrifice, 197
hunter, 88, 89
   big game, 92
hunter-gatherers, 51, 55, 60, 117
   career planning for, 89
   clan groups, 75
hunter-warriors, 163
   and weapons, 147
hunting, bloodless forms of, 89
hunting-gathering, 50
hunting-gathering tribes, 50, 57
   alpha in, 103
   matrilineal, 16
   patrilineal, 16
   predators, 99
hunting territory, 50
hydrogen bomb, 82

IBM, 154, 186
Ifugao, 56
Ik of Central Africa, 137
Ilongot, 56
immunity, 167
In Search of Excellence, 161, 162, 163
Incas, 107
India, 60, 168

industrial tribes, 71, 81
industrialization, 82
inherited wealth, 178
initiations, 141
interpersonal relationships and TV, 69
Iran, 184, 185
Israel, 58
Israelites, 167
ITT, 154, 181
Italy, 107

Japan, 60, 79, 107, 194
Japanese workers, 136
Jay, Anthony, 12, 162
job:
   elimination, 131
   enrichment, 161
   rotation programs, 159
   security, 135
"joining the hunt", 91
jogging, 89
Joseph, 117
Judeo-Christian tradition, 121
Jung, 11, 12, 129, 154

Kalihari, 123, 140
Kennecott, 181
Kennedy, 12, 68, 139
Khomeini, 184, 185
Koppel, Ted, 71
Korea, 82, 192
Krippner, Stanley, 41
! Kung, 93, 94
Kurelu, 32

land ownership, 106
layoffs, 136
leaderless groups, 36
leadership:

quality, 157
skills, 159
visibility, 150, 151
Leakey, Richard, 55
Leary, Timothy, 170
Lebanon, 19
Levi-Strauss, Claude, 54, 88
Lenin, 178
Licensed Consulting Psychologists as headshrinkers, 11
"limited commitment" values, 131
Lindum, the Giver, 56
linking pin, 41
lions, 102
Lorenz, Konrad, 171
loyalty, 134
shallow, 131

machine man, 64, 66
machines, 64, 65
Madison Ave., 154
magic, 104
male:
and female bonding, 45
bonding, 13, 16, 17, 95
clusters, 16
Malinowski, 15, 32, 88, 118
man-of-knowledge, 31, 116, 117, 126
management:
bonus, 34
development, 159
divine rights of, 133
succession, 109
values, 133
manpower planning, 136
market research, 90
marriage(s), 16, 19
Marx, Karl, 12, 175, 177, 178, 182, 184

Marxist, 173, 186
regimes, 188
master bedroom, 83
maternal behavior, 17
matriarchal, 57
"matrix" organizations, 36
Mayans, 195
Maziere, Francis, 121
MBO, 160
McCann-Erickson, 186
McClelland, 108
McKinsey, 161, 186
McLuhan, Marshall, 19, 67, 82
McNeil and Lehrer, 71, 152
Mead, Margaret, 77, 88
"Media Mentors", 71
medicine men, 116
men and women of knowledge, 45
Men in Groups, 12
men's club, 97
Merlin, 117
micro-encephaly, 166
Midianites, 58
military:
analogies, 21
metaphor, 163
missile silos, 195
Mobil, 180
Morison, Samuel Eliot, 52, 53
Mormon missionaries, 122
Morris, Desmond, 168
Moses, 40, 117, 123
mother-child relationships, 17
Mount Olympus, 122
multiple tribal affiliations, 19

Naked Ape, The, 168
Napoleon, 192, 193

Narranganset Indians, 53
nation-states, 19, 57, 79, 84, 163
NBC, 67
Negrito, 56
nepotism, 177
New Guinea, 32, 92
Ngonga, 37, 38
Nicaragua, 193, 194
Nisa, the Life and Words of a !Kung
    Woman, 93
Nixon, 70
nomadic lifestyle, 78
nomadic tribes, 50
nomadism, 74
North Korea, 194
nuclear:
    bombs, 124, 192, 195
    weapons, 168
nurturance and customer
    relationships, 98

office space, 29, 32, 84
Old Testament, 45, 58, 107
Olympics, 68
On the Hana Coast, 59
"ontogeny recapitulates phylogeny", 87
OPEC, 190
organization development, 136
organizations:
    humanistic, 197
    political, 19
organized:
    labor, 133
    religions, 57, 61
Origin of the Family, Private Property
    and the State, 61
Osiris, 56
Ouchi, William, 132

"out to pasture", 152

pack hunting predators, 14
packaging, 90
Page, Martin, 37, 40
partnerships, 22
patriarchal tracing of lineage, 58
patrilineal tribes, 16
payroll, 95
Peace Corps, 118
peasants, 93
pecker heads, 21
pecking order(s), 17, 21, 24, 29, 30,
    31, 32
    and bonus awards, 33
    and division of wealth, 32
    corporate, 84
    in chickens, 24
    in geese, 24
    in universities, 33
    related to territories, 27
peer feedback, 115, 159
People of the Lake, 55
permanent villages, 59
personnel department, 95
Peru, 107
Peters and Waterman, 161
Philippines, 56
pig feasts, 105
Plains Indians, 22
pledges of allegiance, 132
politics and TV, 70
polygamy, 167
Poncas, 54
Pope, the 117
population, 63
    density, 86
power struggles, 136

president, 12, 107
  "hot" with power, 111
priestesses, 96
priests, 116
"prisons collect predators", 96
probationary periods, 156
product:
  design, 90
  manager, 92
production:
  man, 93
  workers as evolved slaves, 148
professional sports, 69
profit:
  goals, 137
  motive, 21
promote from within, 136
prophets, 116, 168
psychological testing, 28
psychologists, 76
  consulting, 116
  management, 157
public accounting, 196
purchasing agents, 92
Pygmies and Dream Giants, 56
pyramid-shaped organization structures,
  36

Quality Circles, 144, 160
quality products, 162
queens, 96

Rasputin, 117
Rather, Dan, 71
Reagan, Ronald, 82, 107, 194
receptionists, 12, 94
Red China, 82
Reich, Charles A., 171
religion, 86, 117

reservation agents, 94, 95, 18
retirement dinners, 144
Rios, Manuel Cordova, 116
rites-of-passage ceremonies, 20, 21
Rome, 59
Russia, 194
Russian pipeline, 82

salaried workers, 34
salaries, 32
salary-to-age ratios, 109
sales:
  clerks, 95
  manager, 92
  meetings as war dances, 139
  regions, 84
  vice presidents, 92
salesman(men), 12, 84, 90, 92
salesmanship, 85
Samoa, 77
Samoans, 122
Satan, 117, 122
Saudi Arabia, 185, 186
Scandinavia, 107
science, 117, 125
scientists, 126
scout, 148
Searle, G. D., 124
SEC, 183
secretaries, 12, 33, 94
seige of Ka-'uiki, 60
self-fulfilling prophecy, 156
serfs, 93
Sesame Street, 67
Severeid, Eric, 71
Shah of Iran, 107, 185
shaman, 11, 88, 116, 126, 148
  corporate, 157

Shostak, Marjorie, 93, 94
shrines for dead chiefs, 29
Sibony, 53
Singer, 180
Sioux Indians, 32, 107, 112, 140
Skinner, B. F., 170
skyscrapers, 49
slash-and-burn farming, 58
slave-labor attitudes, 155
slavemasters, 92
slavery, 79
slaves, 60, 93, 155
small Namba Tribe, 112
small-town farming villages, 75
Social Darwinists, 12
soothsayers, 116
sorceresses, 96
sorceror's apprentice, 148
sororities, 17, 95
South Nias Islanders of Indonesia, 112
sovereignty, 182
Soviet opposition to Polish workers, 178
spatial intelligence, 96
Spenser, Herbert, 12
spirits, 71
Stanley, 51, 81
Stewart, Kilton, 56, 88
stock:
    awards, 156
    holders meeting, 144
    option holders, 34
    options, 32, 156
street gangs, 17
Supreme Court, 70

taboo, 104
    and discussions of salary, 33
    sexual, 121

Tahiti, 107
Taiwan, 180, 188
Tasady, 173
task force projects, 159
Tasmanian Indians, 53
team:
    oriented survival, 83
    spirit, 137
    working, 83
technology, 118
telephone sales, 94
television, 67, 68
    violence, 69
tenant farmers, 93
territorial:
    behavior, 17, 48
    boundaries, 47
    control, 78
    control as male preoccupation, 100
    rules, 45
    sovereignty, 84
    warfare, 51
Territorial Imperative, The, 24, 27, 48
territory, multiple use of, 78
testing, 159
Texaco, 180
Theory X, 159, 160
Theory Z, 132, 160
Third World corporate tribes, 187
Tiano Indians, 52, 53
Tibet, 107
Tierra del Fuego(an), 44, 53
Tiger, Lionel, 12, 13, 16
tigers, 66
Tinbergen, 24
Tippu-Tib, 81
Todas of Tibet, 97
Toffler, Alvin, 169, 170

Togo, 118
torture, 197
Totem and Taboo, 103
Toyotas, 79
trade unions, 177
traffic accidents, 66
training, 95
transportation, 65
tribal:
    affiliation, 132, 155
    analogy, 162
    compound, 50, 94
    costumes, 21
    elders, 31
    heroes, 20
    principles, 45
    regalia, 42
    roles, 11, 87, 144
    roles, evolution of, 88
    shamen, 117
    territory, 47, 74
    warriors, 20
tribe(s):
    Amazon Basin, 16
    American Plains Indians, 122
    Bedouin, 103
    builders, 156
Trobriand Islanders, 15, 32, 118
Turnbull, Colin, 88
TV, 19, 67, 68
    closed circuit, 151
    conditioning, 67
    elders, 71
    heroes, 71
    tribe, 210
    violence, 69, 89
typing pools, 18

Uganda Kob, 24
Union Carbide, 180
unions, 133, 155
United States, 63, 66, 69, 183, 193
    banks, 185
    consumers, 79
    economy, 79
unwritten policies, 28
USSR, 194

Vietnam, 68, 81, 82, 192, 193
Volkswagen, 79
voodoo, 122

walled cities, 61
Wall Street Journal, 137
walruses, 102
war, 80, 86, 191
    weapons of, 84
warlocks, 116
Warwick Castle, 196
Wayne, John, 194
Weatherman, 170
Welby, Marcus, 169
Western New Guinea, 104
Wharton, 148
White Eagle, 54
White House Tapes, 70
William the Conqueror, 59
wise men, 116
witch doctors, 116
witchcraft, 122
wizard(s), 116
    power, 160
women, 18, 101, 147
    exclusion from council huts, 97
    food hunters, 100
    gatherers, 164

    harsh role of, 97
    in sales, 98
World Tribes, 179
World War II, 184, 194
Wukahupi, 104, 105, 106

Yahgan Indians, 53
Yam Factor, The, 37
Yomba of Nigeria, 112
Youngblood, Ron, 59

Zambezi River, 123
Zanzibar, 81
Zenith, 186
Zero-Sum Game, 78

27 million Americans can't read a bedtime story to a child.

It's because 27 million adults in this country simply can't read.

Functional illiteracy has reached one out of five Americans. It robs them of even the simplest of human pleasures, like reading a fairy tale to a child.

You can change all this by joining the fight against illiteracy.

Call the Coalition for Literacy at toll-free **1-800-228-8813** and volunteer.

Volunteer Against Illiteracy.
The only degree you need is a degree of caring.

Ad Council Coalition for Literacy